To Fletcher ♡♡

To Fletcher ♡♡

AN INTRODUCTION TO

DOG CARE

DR SERENA BROWNLIE

THE
APPLE
PRESS

A QUINTET BOOK

Published by Apple Press Ltd.
6 Blundell Street
London N7 9BH

ISBN 1-85076-157-4

This book was designed and produced by
Quintet Publishing Limited
6 Blundell Street
London N7 9BH

Design Director: Peter Bridgewater
Art Director: Ian Hunt
Designer: Nicky Simmonds
Editor: Caroline Beattie
Picture Research: Michael Nicholson

Typeset in Great Britain by
Central Southern Typesetters, Eastbourne
Manufactured in Hong Kong by
Regent Publishing Services Limited
Printed in Hong Kong by
Leefung-Asco Printers Limited

Picture Credits

MARC HENRIE: cover shots, pages 6, 7, 8, 9, 10, 12, 13, 14, 15b,
16, 17, 18, 19, 20, 21, 22b, 23, 24t, 25, 26b, 27, 28t, 29t, 30, 31,
32b, 33, 34t, 36, 37t, 38r, 39t, 40, 41, 42, 44, 45, 46, 48, 51, 53,
54b, 58, 59, 60, 61, 63, 65, 66, 67, 68, 69, 71, 72, 73t, 74, 75, 78,
80, 81, 82, 83, 84, 85, 86, 87, 89, 90l, 92, 94, 95, 96, 97, 98, 100,
101, 103, 104, 105, 107r, 110, 111, 112, 113c, 115, 116, 117,
118 and 120–121.
ARDEA, LONDON: page 73b.
DR SERENA BROWNLIE: pages 79 and 124.
MANDEVILLE VETERINARY HOSPITAL: pages 54t, 90r, 99t, 113t,
106 and 107l.
TERRY SMITH: pages 15t, 22t, 26t, 28b, 29b, 57, 88 and 114.
SPECTRUM COLOUR LIBRARY: pages 24b, 26tr, 34b, 35, 37b, 38l,
39b, 47 and 50.
SALLY ANNE THOMPSON: pages 11, 109, 122 and 125.
BRADLEY VINER: page 113b.
TREVOR WOOD: page 11.

Contents

INTRODUCTION
A New Member of the Household 6

CHAPTER ONE
Acquiring Your Dog 13

CHAPTER TWO
Finding and Choosing Your Puppy 41

CHAPTER THREE
Caring for Your Puppy 46

CHAPTER FOUR
The Growing Dog 57

CHAPTER FIVE
The Adult Dog 72

CHAPTER SIX
Breeding a Litter 88

CHAPTER SEVEN
The Sick or Injured Dog 106

CHAPTER EIGHT
Showing 114

CHAPTER NINE
The Old Dog 122
Index 126

INTRODUCTION

A New Member
of the Household

*A dog can offer invaluable companionship to the
elderly or housebound.*

▲ *Your dog will become an essential part of the family.*

DOG OWNING IS A GREAT JOY but does require commitment. If you have not already acquired a dog but are considering doing so, it is a good idea to think carefully about the advantages and disadvantages.

Dogs are wonderful companions – their love and devotion are legendary, and unconditional. They will continue to love you even if the rest of the world hates you. They share the family's fun, welcome you home, cheer you up when you are sad and offer genuine, wordless comfort in times of grief. The routine of looking after a dog gives a meaning to life for many old or depressed people, and teaches children about responsibility, life

and death and possibly about reproduction. Having to take the dog for a walk in all weathers provides you with exercise, and it is said that stroking a dog may lower your blood pressure. If you are shy your social life may improve – dogs are great ice-breakers and often encourage people to talk to you, especially if you have an unusual breed. You may go to training classes and end up as a showing or obedience enthusiast, in which case you will find yourself with a whole new circle of friends and acquaintances. There are many doggy activities to choose from and it may surprise you to know that most successful owners and breeders on the show circuit or in field trials, agility,

7

A NEW MEMBER OF THE HOUSEHOLD

DOGS AT WORK

The working dog can be trained to perform many invaluable tasks. For example, a dog trained in Scotland to find people buried in snow after avalanches was sent to Mexico and successfully rescued many earthquake victims trapped under the rubble of their homes.

▲▲ *Police dogs in action searching for drugs.*

▶ *Dogs in France are trained to find truffles, elusive delicacies which only grow underground.*

▲ *This Border Collie is helping the shepherd to pen sheep during a sheepdog trial. The routine is an important part of his daily work.*

▶▶ *Dogs are also trained by the military to hunt for explosive devices.*

A NEW MEMBER OF THE HOUSEHOLD

▲ *The blind person's eyes – the guide dog.*

tracking or even dog-sled racing started in a very small way with a family pet. Showing is great fun – you may not often win, but shows would not survive without the amateurs who go along for the pleasure of competing with a much-loved dog.

Of course, dogs have important uses other than as companions. Everyone knows about the dogs which look after blind people, but there are now also hearing dogs for the deaf and 'pat' dogs which are taken to visit old people when they can no longer keep a dog themselves. As working partners, dogs fetch game, gather sheep, catch criminals, sniff out explosives, drugs and people buried in snow. In your home it has been shown that the presence of a dog is one of the most effective burglar deterrents; many dogs will give their lives to protect you.

However, dogs have been the subject of controversy in recent years and dog owners are to blame to a great extent. If allowed out on their own, they can cause road accidents, chase sheep and terrify children. They foul footpaths and parks and this gives rise to understandable fears about infections, but although there are certain diseases which human beings can catch from dogs, most of these diseases are simple to prevent. Parents should keep things in perspective – children are much more likely to be infected by their school chums than they are by their pets.

Owning a dog need not be expensive. Most dogs are not too fussy about what they eat and it is possible to feed even large breeds quite cheaply. The only equipment you really need is a collar and leash and the former should

YOUR DOG AND OTHER PETS

If socialized towards other animals from puppyhood, like the dog and cat here, the dog will cohabit quite happily. If not, his natural instinct as a carnivore, to hunt and catch prey, will prevail.

have a metal disc with your name and telephone number engraved on it, or some other means of identification. In addition you will need grooming equipment for the longer-coated breeds. All dogs appreciate a warm place to sleep, and a blanket in a corner will serve quite well as a bed. The most expensive part of dog-keeping is veterinary fees and it may be worthwhile considering insurance. Third party insurance is also a good idea if you have a large breed dog, in case, despite your precautions, it should escape and cause damage.

Sometimes you may be unlucky and end up with a genuinely difficult dog despite good handling. However, most behavioural problems in dogs are the result of mistakes in training or lack of discipline, therefore the importance of early training cannot be overemphasized. Once a dog has acquired a bad habit, it is very difficult to overcome it later in life, but there are specialists in dog behaviour who can recommend special techniques for solving the problems of naughty dogs.

Many people have said that it is wrong to keep a dog if you do not have a garden. If you are prepared to take the dog out frequently for exercise, and there are no restrictions about pet-keeping in your house or area, then it is quite possible to keep even a large breed dog under these circumstances. However it is worth bearing in mind that a Great Dane, for example, passes a lot of urine and faeces every day and is impossible to carry up and down

four flights of stairs when it is ill or arthritic in old age, even though there were no problems when it could gallop up them by itself. It is lovely to have a large garden if you have a dog but do not imagine that this will mean that you do not have to exercise it. Certainly a dog will run about in the garden if it has another dog to play with, or if it sees the neighbour's cat, but otherwise you may well find it sitting at the door waiting to come back in, or lying asleep in the sun.

Apart from food, water and shelter, the dog's most important requirement is companionship. Although other animals or people may be a substitute, most dogs are only really happy when they are with their owners. The more independent ones can adjust to being left alone for long periods especially if accustomed to it when young, but some dogs become bored or even frantic when their owners are absent, resulting in destructiveness and constant barking. Of course no-one can take a dog with them everywhere, and training to be good when left in the house or car is important for every puppy. However as a potential owner you should realize that dog owning is not practical if you work long hours or go on frequent trips away from home unless you are able to take the dog along.

Holiday time is also a problem as boarding kennels are quite expensive and your relatives may not always be keen to help out, therefore you may be forced to take

A NEW MEMBER OF THE HOUSEHOLD

▲ *A walk in the countryside – vital exercise for your dog and an opportunity for the family to enjoy a healthy and relaxing pursuit.*

your dog with you. This can be great fun, however, as dogs also enjoy a holiday, and it is not too difficult to find hotels and guesthouses which will accept a well-behaved dog. If the proprietor refuses, it is usually because a previous guest left a mess behind him, therefore every owner should realize that others will suffer as a result of carelessness. If you are fortunate you will find that a few hotel owners prefer dogs to children for the same reasons!

There is one last point to consider. It would be heartbreaking to have to part with a dog once you have acquired it because you did not realize that a member of your family is allergic to dogs. It is not fair to ask a breeder to give you a puppy on trial as it will be more difficult to resell and the puppy itself may be upset by changes of environment, therefore it is a good idea to visit friends with dogs, or to offer to look after one for a short period.

Now that you know what is involved, the next stage is to decide what sort of dog you would like, whether you want a dog or a bitch and then to choose one. It is important to make the right decision as the average dog lives for 10 to 15 years. Your own circumstances may alter in that time but dogs are fairly adaptable. There is no doubt that dog-owning is addictive and the chances are that once you have known the love a dog can give you, you will never want to be without one.

You have been warned!

CHAPTER ONE

Acquiring your Dog

*The Toy Poodle – lively and smart – requires
regular sessions at the grooming parlour to
maintain this traditional clipped shape.*

ACQUIRING YOUR DOG

DOG OR BITCH?

This is a difficult question to answer as it depends very much on your own temperament and circumstances. Many first-time owners choose a dog because they do not want the bother of looking after a bitch in season or the financial outlay of having her neutered (spayed). Certainly if you live in a house with no garden and have to take the dog for walks, a bitch in season will soon cause trouble in the neighbourhood as dogs will congregate around the door waiting for her to come out! However, if you do have a garden you need not take her out and you may find that the local dogs do not even realize that she is in season. New owners also worry about the mess but usually there is surprisingly little bloody discharge and the bitch will do her best to keep clean by licking. If you have a large breed, the bitches are often quieter and easier to handle, though some people say they are not so affectionate or so playful. Dog owners have to be careful with other males in case of fights and the dog may wander after bitches. It is all a matter of personal preference.

WHICH BREED?

You may already have decided on the type of dog you want. You may have been influenced by dogs owned by relatives or friends, by the breed your family owned when you were a child or one that you have admired on television. Some people are equally dedicated to the idea of owning a crossbred dog, believing them to be healthier. A crossbred is certainly likely to be less expensive to buy, but it will be no less expensive to keep.

However, if you are not sure which breed you want, there are certain points to consider and these are size, temperament, food and exercise requirements, ease of coat care and special requirements, e.g., good with children, or a good guard.

Dog breeds come in all sizes from very tiny to very large indeed and they can be divided into categories depending on the function for which they were originally bred.

THE TOY BREEDS

The toy breeds, weighing usually less than 11 lb (5 kg) and possibly less than 4.4 lb (2 kg), make delightful pets for the small town house or apartment and are suitable companions for older people. Despite their small size, they are usually very lively and full of fun, but they are easily injured and young children may not realize this. They eat more for their size (relatively) than large dogs but not a great quantity. However they may be quite

▲ *The Long-coated Chihuahua.*

▲ *One of the most popular toy breeds – a Yorkshire Terrier bitch and puppies.*

▲ *A Maltese Terrier's coat requires frequent attention to keep it looking as good as this.*

▲ *A Papillon family group with attractive symmetrical markings and the typical 'butterfly' ears.*

choosy and often prefer their owner's food to dog food! They may be difficult to house train but pass only small quantities of waste material anyway, so hygiene is not usually a problem. They are surprisingly undaunted as a rule by large dogs and may get themselves into trouble! Unfortunately some breeds have a few inherent veterinary problems because of their size.

▲ *The Pomeranian – a tiny toy breed with Spitz characteristics.*

There are some well-known examples of toys. The vivacious Toy Poodle is lively and very intelligent, with a wavy coat which does not moult but does need clipping to keep it tidy. (Poodles come in three sizes: Toy, Miniature and Standard.) The Chihuahua is characterized by its very round skull, high-stepping action and impudent character and comes in long- and short-coated varieties. The dimunitive Yorkshire Terrier has a long silky coat and looks very sweet sitting on a cushion, but this is still a terrier with plenty of spirit. Not all of this breed are tiny and larger specimens can still be found. This is also true of the fluffy Pomeranian and the larger ones are similar to the other Spitz breeds to be described later. Another small terrier is the Maltese which also has a long, silky coat, pure white this time. Rather less well-known is the Papillon, a lovely little dog so named because of its large 'butterfly' ears. Some of the slightly larger breeds are also classified with the toys for show purposes as their original function was to be companions, e.g., the Pekinese and the Cavalier King Charles Spaniel.

If you would feel uncomfortable walking in the street with a tiny dog, you may prefer something bigger.

THE TERRIERS

Terriers were bred for hunting and killing vermin, by flushing them out of holes and thick cover. Even though they vary in appearance, all the breeds in this group still have the kind of temperament which enabled them to do their job – lively, keen and intelligent, capable of lightning reactions and with a tendency to belligerence, especially towards other dogs. They need firm handling from puppyhood and even though they may be very good-natured, young children should be prevented from taking any liberties with them. Examples of popular breeds which originated from Scotland are the short-legged West Highland White, Cairn, Skye and Scottish Terriers (usually called 'Scotties') and the longer-legged Border Terrier, a charming little dog with an otter-like expression. From England came the Fox Terrier (Smooth or Wire-haired), the strong, pugnacious Bull Terrier and Staffordshire Bull Terrier, the tall tan and black Airedale, which has been used sometimes as a police dog and the Airedale's smaller version, the Lakeland Terrier. Less common are the red Norwich and Norfolk terriers, very similar apart from the former having prick ears, and the unusual looking Bedlington Terrier, which has a close curly coat making it look rather like a lamb. The very

▲ *A Border Terrier bitch and puppy.*

▲ *A lovely black Scottish Terrier – a big dog on short legs with very powerful jaws.*

ACQUIRING YOUR DOG

▲ *A Wire-haired Fox Terrier at his most alert.*

▲ *The Norfolk Terrier is often confused with the prick-eared Norwich.*

▲ *An unusual terrier – the curly-coated Bedlington.*

▲ *A Lakeland Terrier.*

▲ *The Boston – a terrier with Bulldog characteristics.*

▲ *This Bull Terrier looks unusually quiet, but she shows the typical roman nose or 'downface'.*

ACQUIRING YOUR DOG

▲ *The Australian Terrier – not quite as well known as the longer coated Silky.*

▲ *The popular Jack Russell Terrier.*

▲ *The Chow-Chow showing the typical 'blue' tongue.*

popular but unrecognized Jack Russell Terrier was bred originally by an English parson and is widely used for ratting and as a hunt terrier. From Wales comes the Welsh Terrier, from Ireland the red Irish Terrier along with the more powerful grey-black Kerry Blue, and from Australia the Australian Silky.

Care of the coat is an important consideration when choosing a terrier, as you will need professional assistance with trimming unless you obtain tuition in doing it yourself. Terriers are generally tough, hardy dogs but certain breed-specific diseases are recognized.

THE SPITZ BREEDS

The type of dog known as Spitz shows variation in size, colour and coat length but all the Spitz breeds have the same basic head and body shape, with the tail usually curled over the back. Since most came from countries with cold climates, they have weather-resisting double coats, consisting of a short woolly undercoat and longer, outer guard hairs. They were bred for a variety of purposes – for companionship, herding, hunting, guarding and draught work. Although they may not be given the

ACQUIRING YOUR DOG

▲ *A Norwegian Elkhound showing typical coat and markings.*

▲ *The smiling face of a beautiful champion Samoyed bitch.*

▲ *The Siberian Husky – built for speed and stamina in the harshest conditions.*

▲ *An Alaskan Malamute in an unusual colour – most are wolf-grey and white.*

▲ *A superb Finnish Spitz.*

23

ACQUIRING YOUR DOG

▲ *One of the smaller members of the Spitz group – the Norwegian Buhund.*

▲ *A lovely pair of Japanese Spitz.*

opportunity to perform their original tasks, the Spitz breeds are probably the most 'primitive' dogs in temperament, being aloof, independent and having the reputation of being difficult to train. However, they can also be extremely faithful and affectionate to their owners and are usually very good with children. With other dogs, the pack instinct is strong and fights may occur unless dominance is established. The larger members of the group cannot be trusted with farm livestock unless used to them from an early age. Some breeds have a tendency to be noisy – this is worth bearing in mind if you have touchy neighbours! Some larger examples of the Spitz type are the Eskimo dog, the Siberian Husky and the Alaskan Malamute which were bred for draught purposes, the beautiful white Samoyed, originally from northern Russia, which herded reindeer, the Norwegian Elkhound, grey, black and white in colour, and the striking Japanese Akita. Slightly smaller are the Keeshond, bred to guard the

barges on the Dutch canals, the red Finnish Spitz, the Norwegian Buhund, the Chow from China, and, smaller still, the white Japanese Spitz and the Pomeranian. Show Pomeranians are very tiny and classed as toys but, like the Yorkie, they were bred down from larger specimens. Problems with Spitz breeds arise, as with terriers, in handling the males of the larger breeds and in coping with the longer coat types, but generally Spitz dogs are pretty healthy apart from one or two diseases recognized in particular breeds. They have one great advantage as house dogs – they have very little 'doggy' odour.

THE SHEPHERD DOGS

If you are looking for a dog which is easier to train, e.g., for obedience work, you may choose one of the sheep or cattle dog types. They are willing, faithful, anxious to please and very hard-working – in fact these dogs have a

▲ *A tricolour Rough Collie.*

25

▲ *The ever-popular German Shepherd Dog.*

▲ *Hungarian Pulis.*

▲ *The Border Collie is bred as a working dog.*

▲ *A young Old English Sheepdog.*

real need to work and some may become temperamentally unstable if the owner is not prepared to give them plenty of exercise and something to occupy their minds! Since sheepdogs were and are used to protect the flocks, they are also usually good guards. Some examples of this type are very well-known – the German Shepherd Dog (formerly known as the Alsatian), now more commonly used as a police or guide dog, the Border Collie, a hardy, long-lived breed capable of covering enormous distances in the course of a day's work, the Rough Collie (remember Lassie?) and the Shetland Sheepdog (a small version of the Rough Collie). Other examples not quite so well-known are the Belgian Shepherd Dog which comes in several varieties, the long-coated Bearded Collie, the Australian Kelpie and the unusual Eastern European breeds such as the Hungarian Puli and Komondor with their curious corded coats. Another sheepdog which is a great favourite is the Old English, but this large dog with its lumbering gait, very heavy coat and rather phlegmatic nature would probably find sheep-herding rather diffi-

cult in its present-day form! The Corgi also belongs in this category as it was once used as a cattle dog.

Veterinary problems are not widespread in this group apart from the German Shepherd Dog and Old English, which have suffered from the effects of overbreeding.

▲ *A pretty Pembroke Corgi.*

▲ *The ultimate guard dog – a male Rotweiler is heavier than the average man.*

▲ *The Boxer.*

THE **G**UARDING **B**REEDS

If you require a pet which was also bred mainly as a guard dog your choice might be a Dobermann Pinscher, a Rottweiler or a Boxer. These are examples of breeds which have the reputation of being very fierce with strangers but are devoted to their owners. They may be very boisterous when young, and need firm discipline, especially the males. It is important to remember that, unless you live in a castle on an island, your dog will have to be socially acceptable and should not be a danger to anyone in everyday situations – the ideal guard dog is friendly towards everyone unless on guard. The breeds mentioned are short-coated which reduces grooming but unfortunately veterinary attention is often needed, particularly for younger Rottweilers because of orthopaedic problems and for older Boxers which, for reasons not understood, seems to be particularly prone to cancer.

GUNDOGS

Dogs have been bred to assist people with shooting small game in a variety of ways. They will find suitable wild animals and birds, flush them out of undergrowth and

▲ *The English Springer Spaniel makes an excellent all-purpose gun dog.*

bushes and then retrieve them once shot. Each breed had a specific purpose but some will perform all these tasks. To be suitable for the job, a dog has to be energetic, eager to please and capable of being trained to a high standard of obedience. He must have a very well-developed sense of smell and not grip too hard when carrying game – a good gundog will carry an egg without breaking it. He does not have to be particularly faithful to one person as he would be required to work for several, and therefore has to be friendly towards everyone. He must not be afraid of loud noises or become excited or distracted by animals other than those of interest to the owner, and so he should have a steady, calm temperament. These attributes make gundogs very good pets, guide dogs and 'sniffer' dogs for explosives or drugs.

Now for examples. Everyone knows the popular gentle Golden Retriever, the happy Labrador Retriever which may be yellow, black or chocolate in colour, the long-eared Cocker Spaniel, the smallest of the gundogs, and the larger liver and white English Springer Spaniel. Other varieties of spaniel include the red and white Welsh Springer, the now rare Clumber spaniel and Sussex spaniel, the profuse-coated American Cocker and the Brittany spaniel. The King Charles and Cavalier King

▲ *Two beautiful Golden Retrievers.*

▲ *A yellow Labrador Retriever.*

▲ *An American Cocker Spaniel.*
◄ *Two Welsh Springer Spaniels.*

Charles spaniels are very old breeds which, though they have the delightful soft temperament of the gundog, were bred to be companions rather than workers. The setters and pointers also belong to the gundog group – the most common is the Irish Setter, an elegant dog with a glorious red chestnut silky coat, but the English Setter, characterized by a mainly white coat with coloured hairs giving a roan appearance and the large black and tan Gordon Setter should not be forgotten. In addition to the English Pointer, there are several pointer-type breeds with shortened tails, such as the German Short Haired Pointer, the striking grey-fawn Weimeraner and the russet red Hungarian Vizsla which may be good all-round gundogs.

In general all the dogs in this group are easy to keep and grooming is not usually a problem except for the Cocker and American Cocker which have long dense hair on the legs and ears. Labradors are extremely greedy as a rule and they must not be too well fed unless working hard. Veterinary problems are usually associated with the

AN INTRODUCTION TO DOG CARE

ACQUIRING YOUR DOG

▲ *The largest of the setters – the Gordon.*

▲ *A Weimaraner at work.*

▲ *The Hungarian Vizla.*

type of life the dog leads, such as picking up thorns and grass seeds, but the popular breeds do have certain inherited conditions.

THE HOUNDS

Dogs of this group were bred to hunt down animals by outrunning them, either for food for their owners or for sport. Many of these breeds are very old. They may hunt singly or in packs, either by following a trail by scent or by sprinting after prey that they follow by sight. The characteristics of a good hound, therefore, are speed, agility and stamina, along with a certain independence of mind since it cannot rely on its owner in a tight situation. Though they rarely work nowadays, all hounds retain their urge to chase – cats, small dogs and rabbits beware – and they will escape if they can to indulge this instinct. However, with humans they are usually gentle, quiet and easy to handle. Many people wish to own a sight hound because of their beauty – the glorious long flowing coat of the Afghan, the graceful movement of the Saluki, the powerful elegance of the Borzoi. The Greyhound is often only considered as a racing machine, but when their racing days are over these lovely dogs often end up looking for a home and can make very good pets. If a Greyhound is too big, you might consider the smaller but similar Whippet or the tiny Italian Greyhound.

The scent hounds are noted for character. The tracking dog *par excellence* is of course the Bloodhound, with its sad expression, folds of skin and long droopy ears. The Basset Hound has even longer ears, with a long body to match and can muster a fair turn of speed on its short, stubby legs. The smaller member of the family, more commonly kept as a pet, is the Beagle and, sadly this

▲ *Like a pair of bearded wizards, two Afghan Hounds in a medieval setting.*

▲ *The elegant Borzoi.*

ACQUIRING YOUR DOG

▲ *A Bassett Hound with the typical, rather doleful expression.*

▲ *A pack of Foxhounds at the meet.*

ACQUIRING YOUR DOG

▲ *The supreme canine racing machine – the Greyhound.*

breed is also widely used as a laboratory animal because they are a convenient size and easy to keep and breed. However, packs of Beagles still hunt in the countryside like their larger cousins, the Foxhounds.

THE SHORT-NOSED (BRACHYCEPHALIC) BREEDS

This type of dog has many devotees, though they cannot really be called beautiful. However, these dogs have great character and the snuffling noises that they make are quite endearing. The most famous example of this group is the courageous and strong British Bulldog, bred for bull-baiting although its lumbering gait may make this hard to imagine. Much smaller is the French Bulldog, which has prick ears, the black and white Boston Terrier and the Pug. Noses come in varying degrees of shortness but one of the flattest faces of all belongs to the little Pekinese with its profuse harsh coat. Almost as flat is the face of the Tibetan breed, the Shih-Tzu, another small, short-legged breed with a long silky coat. Much less short-faced are the larger Tibetan breeds, the Lhasa Apso and the charming Tibetan Spaniel which, though it may be mistken for a Pekinese, is as a rule much more robust and is more similar in character to a Spitz.

Although they are very lovable, it must be said that the very flat-nosed breeds have been produced by selective breeding over the years for what is in fact an abnormality.

Many may live for years with no veterinary problems but even the healthiest do have difficulty breathing and the worst affected many actually suffocate in hot weather or need corrective surgery. Therefore they are perhaps best avoided by the first-time dog owner.

▲ *The Pug is a well-known short-nosed breed.*

▲ *The Bulldog – traditional symbol of British courage and tenacity – guarding his garden.*

▲ *The Shih-Tzu – a small breed of Tibetan origin with a long flowing coat.*

▲ *A particolour Tibetan Spaniel. These charming, independent little dogs make excellent pets and are very long-lived.*

▲ *The Pekingese has the flattest nose of all short-nosed breeds.*

▲ *Two St Bernards.*

THE GIANT BREEDS

No one buys a giant breed dog unless they are prepared to reorganize their lives around it. They are expensive pets to buy, and to rear, and veterinary treatment costs more – the bigger the dog the more drugs they require. You may end up buying a bigger car to accommodate it and even perhaps a bigger house, and at the end of it all you may only have had the pleasure of owning it for seven or eight years, because these dogs are not long-lived. Yet most people who have owned a giant breed dog will go through it all again with another, because no smaller dog can take its place. The giant dog must have a good temperament – it would be extremely dangerous if it did not – and most are very gentle and quiet. Although they need a large quantity of food while growing, their adult intake may be surprisingly low and they need much less exercise than the average gundog or collie. Because they are so strong, they must be trained to walk properly on a leash when young and not to bowl people over in enthusiastic greeting! The main problems arise if they become ill, since nursing is difficult and physically de-manding, and, sadly, they are prone to many disease conditions.

Popular examples are the Great Dane, a tall, imposing yet graceful dog, the St Bernard, traditionally bred to assist stranded mountain travellers in Switzerland, and

the other Mountain dog, the white Pyrenean. From the cold East Coast of Canada, the black Newfoundland also has a thick, weather-resisting coat. The Irish Wolfhound and slightly smaller Scottish Deerhound are the largest members of the hound group, capable of considerable speed despite their size. In contrast, the huge Mastiff does not need to move very fast to protect his owner's property – who would risk upsetting him?

▲ *The Irish Wolfhound – a gentle giant.*

THE CROSSBRED DOG

It is impossible to imagine a type of crossbred dog which has not been produced at some time or another, usually resulting from an unintentional mating. It is said that crossbreds are healthier than pure-breds but this is not necessarily true. Certainly it is recognized that mating together two totally unrelated animals tends to produce more vigorous progeny than continually mating close relatives, but if one parent has an inherited defect or disease it will pass it on whatever the other parent is. Also it must not be assumed that crossbred dogs have more resistance to infectious diseases. If you have seen both parents then it is usually easy to imagine what your cross-bred puppy may look like when it grows up, but if the parents were themselves crossbred, the result will be a complete lottery! Some guide to eventual size may be gained from looking at the size of a puppy's paws but this is notoriously unreliable. The other question mark is often temperament – it should be possible to assess this more accurately if the parents are known. For these reasons, it may be advisable to choose a young adult dog if you want to be sure of a particular type.

▲ *The Pyrenean Mountain dog has a thick weather-resistant coat.*

▲ *A lovely example of the majestic Great Dane.*

▲ 'Lurcher' is often used for any Greyhound cross but is
correctly reserved for a Greyhound & Irish Wolfhound.

▲ A most attractive shaggy crossbred, with perhaps
Bearded Collie somewhere in his pedigree.

▲ This gentle-looking crossbred's dam or sire was probably a black Labrador.

CHAPTER TWO

Finding and Choosing Your Puppy

Caring for a young puppy requires endless patience, but can be a delightfully rewarding experience.

FINDING A PEDIGREE PUPPY

Anyone can be a dog breeder provided that they own a Kennel Club-registered bitch of breeding age. However if you are buying a puppy it is always best to go to a reputable source, someone to whom you can return for advice if there are problems later. A breeder who cares about his or her reputation will ensure that their puppies are healthy and well-reared. If you are interested in showing, the breeder will also do his or her best to ensure you're being sold a show-quality puppy, although no one can predict that a pup will become a champion. A very well-known breeder who has a large number of dogs may have a puppy available straightaway but usually you must be prepared to put your name down on a waiting list. It is much better to wait a while for a good puppy than to buy one in a hurry and regret it later. You will probably be surprised by the breeder's approach to you. You may have to answer questions about the facilities you have at home, and it has been known for a breeder to refuse to sell a puppy if he or she considers a prospective buyer unsuitable. The last thing a breeder wants is to have the puppy returned, but the caring breeder would prefer you to return it than to try to sell it to someone else. You will be given a diet sheet to follow and advice on rearing and training. Of course you should also obtain a copy of the pedigree and any registration documents, insurance and vaccination certificates, if available.

The best way of contacting reputable breeders is to telephone or write to the main governing body of dog breeding and showing, the Kennel Club, and the staff will give you a list of names and addresses of well-known breeders and secretaries of breed clubs. The club secretaries usually know who has puppies available and if there are any in your area. However, you should be prepared to travel a considerable distance for the right puppy. Another method of contacting breeders is to attend dog shows, walk round the benches and talk to people, or you can obtain copies of the dog newspapers and breed journals – some breeders will advertise in these. A third method, the one that most first-time buyers use, is to scan the advertisements in your local newspaper. This is much less reliable as you have no guarantee how experienced the advertisers are, but of course it is still possible to obtain a nice, well-reared puppy from a pet bitch with a good pedigree.

Pedigree puppies may also be obtained from pet shops and dealers. However, many buyers have suffered financial loss and heartbreak from these sources. If the

◀ *Rottweiler puppies may look very endearing, but the breed requires careful training.*

FINDING AND CHOOSING YOUR PUPPY

▲ *Children and puppies share a natural curiosity and playfulness, but do supervise their play.*

puppies were not bred on the premises, they may have been transported hundreds of miles in unsuitable conditions and exposed to disease. At best they will be nervous, confused and suffer stomach upsets from dietary changes. At worst they will be parasite-ridden, incubating disease or even dying. Even the inexperienced purchaser should be able to spot puppies in poor condition. Remember 'caveat emptor' – 'let the buyer beware'.

FINDING A CROSSBRED PUPPY

Although there are undoubtedly far too many dogs in Britain, many of them unwanted, setting out to find a healthy crossbred puppy may be more difficult than you think. Most people obtain one from friends whose bitch 'got out when she was in season' or from an advertisement in the local paper or pet shop window. Your local vet should know of pups in the area if he has attended the whelping, but many bitches whelp without assistance. If you buy a puppy in a pet shop, the same remarks apply regarding parasites and diseases as to pedigree puppies. It is a noble gesture to buy one from one of the animal charities or dogs' homes. Nowadays they are careful to vaccinate every dog as soon as it arrives and they do try to sell only healthy puppies, but you must be prepared emotionally and financially for disease problems developing as their background is unknown.

CHOOSING YOUR PUPPY

Once you have contacted your breeder and made an appointment to choose your puppy you will need to know what to look for. It is very exciting for children to be allowed to go along but do not be surprised if the breeder will not permit the children to handle the puppies – it is not unknown for a puppy to be killed or injured by being dropped. You may be asked to remove your shoes and outer clothes as the puppies will probably be unvaccinated.

The time between three and six weeks of age is very vital to a puppy because it is during this time that its behaviour towards humans is established. Careful breeders will ensure that puppies are handled as much as possible – this is known as 'socializing'. Puppies living in the house will probably be better socialized than those living in kennels but there should not be too much difference. Well-socialized puppies will be friendly and outgoing – if you sit down among them they will soon be crawling all over you and chewing your clothes, unless they are all fast asleep after a meal, in which case it is better to wait a little while rather than try to wake them up. If there is one that seems to be particularly shy, it is best avoided, since it will require knowledgeable and sympathetic handling later. Also beware the big pup which is bullying all the rest – it may try to bully you too! If you want a show pup, you can either take the breeder's advice or take along a friend who knows something about the breed. You may be unfortunate and find that there is only one puppy available because all the rest are sold – if it looks small and thin, pot-bellied or deformed in any way, do not buy it. Most breeders will be happy to allow you to take the puppy to a vet for a check-up but it is only fair to do this straightaway so that it can be returned immediately if something is wrong. You should be able to see the mother, and if you are lucky the sire as well, but remember that a bitch which has reared a big litter may look in poor condition despite good feeding, and will be losing her coat.

Once you have chosen your puppy, you will want to take it home. Pups of the bigger breeds should not leave the nest until six weeks and those of the small breeds may not be ready to go until eight weeks or later. If you have to wait, you can fill in the time buying food, bowls, a blanket, a little collar and a basket if you decide to use one (make sure it is made of a fairly indestructible material). You might also visit your friends collecting supplies of newspaper – you are going to need it!

Transporting the puppy is best done by car. Take along your blanket and some tissues as the pup may be car-sick. During a long journey a little water should be offered or perhaps milk, but the puppy may be sick if given food. If very long distances are involved it may be worth considering flying – the breeder may have an airline crate which can be returned, and puppies are surprisingly unconcerned by this mode of travel.

TAKING ON AN OLDER DOG

You may feel that because of your circumstances you could take on an adult dog but do not have the time or the energy to cope with a puppy.

Once you have made the decisions about the sex and breed you want, you have several avenues to explore and you should not have to pay very much.

Firstly you may approach a breeder. As stated previously, reputable breeders will always try to take back a dog that they have bred when the owners can no longer keep it, or if they have a large number of dogs, they may be prepared to part with a bitch which is too old for breeding or a young dog which did not fulfil show expectations. If you have no luck there, the breed club secretaries will give you names and addresses of the big-hearted people (there are some in every breed) who run the 'rescue service'. They keep registers of dogs and bitches looking for new homes and there are usually plenty of them, especially in the large breeds. You may not be given a pedigree with a 'rescue dog' but most people are not worried about this.

Secondly, especially if you want a crossbred, you can contact the animal charities and dogs' homes – there are

▲ *These food and water bowls are perhaps a little large for this Poodle pup.*

literally millions of nice dogs looking for new homes every year and most will be put to sleep if homes are not found. Pedigree dogs end up in charity kennels also in surprising numbers. Once again you must be prepared to accept the risk of disease developing.

Thirdly, as for puppies, newspaper advertisements may reveal a suitable animal.

Wherever the dog comes from, you should be prepared to ask some searching questions about the animal's past history, and if this is unknown, as with a stray, the only thing you can do is to try to persuade the seller to let you have the dog on a short trial basis. It is most unwise to take on a dog with known problems, either veterinary or behavioural. Dogs with doubtful temperaments should be put to sleep rather than rehomed. Those which have learned to be very destructive will probably not change their ways when rehomed, although if it has been left alone all day previously you might consider giving it a chance. However, there are plenty of dogs which have to be rehomed through no fault of their own. Do not reject an older dog if it appears to be in good health. Dogs which have lived in a kennel all their lives may not adapt well to house-living and will not be house-trained but if you are prepared to be patient, your efforts may be rewarded.

If you already have one dog and wish to obtain another, this raises additional problems. Bitches are much less inclined to fight but those of the terrier breeds particularly may do so. Male dogs will very often fight, and may continue to do so if neither is much more dominant than the other. Most older dogs will accept a puppy, but once the puppy grows up and becomes sexually mature, a fight may ensue over something trivial and will continue. If this situation occurs there is no cure and one dog must go. When introducing two adult dogs for the first time it is better to do so when out for a walk, on neutral territory.

CHAPTER THREE

Caring for Your

Puppy

Beware the inclination of all puppies to chew
any available object!

SETTLING IN

Your puppy will be cold and lonely on his first night away from his dam and littermates. Comfort him by placing a warm hot-water bottle, wrapped in a blanket, in his bed.

THE FIRST NIGHT

A puppy's first night in a new home is a traumatic experience – for owner as well as puppy. You will both be tired if you have had a long journey and the puppy may be frightened, though if he had an outgoing personality before, you will be astonished at how quickly he will regain confidence.

Food is first on the agenda. A puppy of six weeks will need five small meals a day; one of eight weeks, four meals a day. When you arrive home, the puppy will be hungry. Ideally the breeder may have given you some of the puppy's regular food to take home. If not, a little minced meat (2–4 oz) with a tablespoonful of puppy biscuit (soaked) will do to begin with, as most puppies will eat this readily. While you are preparing this meal, confine the puppy to a small area of one room, usually the kitchen, with some newspaper on the floor. As soon as the puppy relaxes, he will want to pass urine and if he has not done so already, he will certainly want to after eating. If you have a garden, decide which part is to be the puppy's toilet area and take him out as soon as he has finished eating. You will need to stay with the puppy to make sure he does not wander too far, but as soon as he squats down, praise him lavishly and carry him back inside. However if he does urinate indoors do not scold him – you will have plenty of opportunities to try this exercise

later! After eating, the dog will probably want to play a little and this is your chance to get to know your new puppy. You will probably have bought him a few toys – squeaky rubber ones are popular but watch that he does not take the squeaker out and swallow it! A rubber ring or a ball (big enough so that the puppy cannot choke on it) will be chased and cow-hide chews are useful for exercising those needle-sharp teeth! His energy will not last for long and very soon he will collapse in a corner in a little sleepy heap. At this stage you may put it to bed and tiptoe off to have a well-earned meal yourself.

Once the puppy wakes up, the first thing he will do is urinate, therefore you should pick him up and take him outside. Mission accomplished, he should be ready for supper – a milky drink and perhaps a baby biscuit. Young puppies do not usually have strong enough jaws to cope with dog biscuits at this stage. He will need a dish of water for through the night, although he may well paddle in it, plenty of newspapers all over the floor will be required. When you are ready for bed, fill a hot water bottle and wrap it in a blanket for the puppy's bed. It may also be a good idea to leave a ticking clock in the room – the puppy will miss his dam and littermates when alone, so warmth and a soothing noise may help him get to sleep. When you retire to your bedroom, initially there will be plaintive cries and heartbreaking howls. It is most unwise to give in and go back to the puppy – having

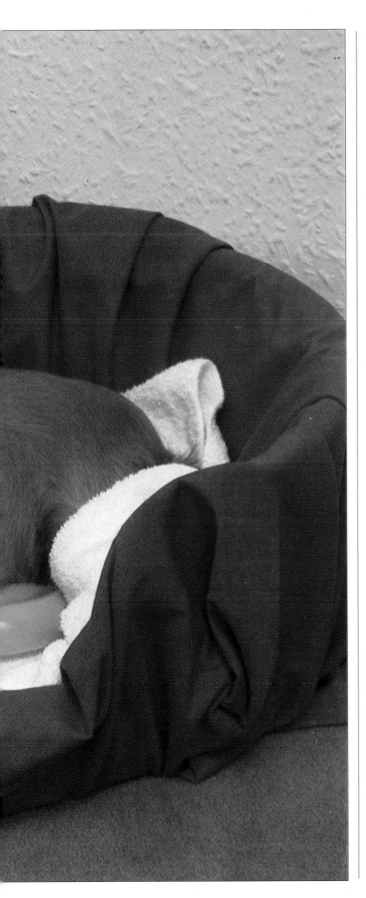

succeeded in attracting your attention he will simply repeat the process and neither of you will sleep much. The only exception to this is if you hear shrieks of pain, of course – you will know the difference! It is wise to leave him in a room which is as safe as possible, with no small spaces in which it may become trapped.

Next morning you will come down to quite a mess – dirty wet papers may be strewn everywhere if you have a large puppy. If you persevere with house-training this will soon diminish, although you cannot expect the dog to be clean during the night for some time.

THE DAILY ROUTINE AND FEEDING

Like any baby, routine is important and you will realize by now that puppy-rearing is almost a full-time job. Fortunately, unlike human babies, this period of intensive work is short and after about three months, the puppy should be able to fit in more with your lifestyle than vice versa.

You will find that the routine develops as follows: Clear up papers and replace with fresh, Breakfast, Garden, Play, Sleep, Garden, Play, Lunch, Garden, etc.

If you have to take the puppy to work, leaving him in the car is possible, provided you can attend to him regularly. Even so it is very advisable to arrange to be on holiday for the first two weeks at least.

For the first week or so, you should stick to the breeder's diet sheet but then the situation should be reassessed, with assistance from your vet. Quantities of food have to be increased gradually as the puppy grows, and if the diet is unsuitable, any changes should also be made gradually to avoid stomach upsets. You have the choice of using a home-prepared diet from ingredients which you buy yourself, or using a commercial puppy food. Some people have objections to using canned or packet food for dogs believing it to be inferior to fresh food. However, it is important to remember that food manufacturers spend a great deal of money on research to make sure that their foods contain everything a growing puppy needs and there is a real risk that a home-prepared diet may be deficient in several vital components, particularly calcium. Commercially prepared foods may be dry, though they are best fed soaked with water or gravy, semi-moist or canned. The dry and semi-moist foods are usually complete whereas the canned meats are intended to be mixed with puppy biscuit. The manufacturers print instructions on the packet or can to tell you how much to give, but to be safe they tend to overestimate require-

◀ *An inviting and comfortable bed has been made for this English Cocker Spaniel puppy.*

▲ *These Keeshund puppies have quickly mastered the technique of eating from a bowl. If your puppy is a fussy eater it may be due to lack of competition.*

▶ *If handled properly, your puppy should be well socialized and outgoing like these blue roan Cocker Spaniels.*

ments, therefore adjust the quantities according to your puppy's appetite. If the puppy is very greedy, too much food will give him diarrhoea and tend to make him fat, whereas if he is given too little, he will be constantly hungry, crying for food and will not grow properly. Unfortunately no one can lay down hard and fast rules about quantities – it is something you have to judge by trial and error.

For those who decide to use a home-prepared diet, the following suggestions may be helpful. The quantities are those for an eight-week old puppy whose adult weight will be about 50 lb (22.5 kg).

■ **BREAKFAST** – 2 tbs (30 ml) cereal mixed with ¼ pt (120 ml) of milk.

■ **MIDDAY** – 4 oz minced meat (ground beef), 2 tbs (30 ml) puppy biscuit (soaked) + half the recommended daily dose of a proprietary mineral/vitamin supplement.

■ **DINNER** – as above or replace meat with one egg (scrambled), canned tuna, fish, chicken, rabbit, cottage cheese or tripe. Other offal may be given occasionally but it tends to cause diarrhoea, especially liver.

■ **SUPPER** – as breakfast, or milky rice pudding, custard or milk with baby rusks (baby biscuits).

For the large breeds extra bone meal will do no harm but cod-liver oil should be avoided or given at most once weekly as too much vitamin D can be dangerous. A small amount of vegetable oil, e.g., corn oil is good for the skin and coat (1 tsp daily).

HOUSE TRAINING

If you have the time to devote to your puppy and take him out to his garden toilet area frequently you will soon find that you recognize the signs when the puppy wants to urinate or pass a motion. He will become slightly agitated and squeaky, tending to walk in circles. When he comes to you and rushes to the door, you have won the battle but the time taken to achieve this is remarkably variable. Males tend to be easier to house-train than females, and those of the large breeds easier than the small breeds. Even when you thought you had succeeded, accidents will still happen – never scold a puppy unless you actually catch him in the act, because he will only relate punishment to what he is doing at the time, not to something five minutes earlier. It is no surprise that summer puppies will be house-trained more quickly than winter puppies. They often want a game outside before they will capitulate and perform – who wants to stand in the garden in freezing wind and rain while the puppy dances around apparently oblivious to the weather? Of course, they will produce the goods immediately after coming back inside – if only you had stayed outside a few minutes longer! Staying with the puppy is vital, not only to see that the deed has been done, but also to remove from his mouth all the stones, twigs and plants he will try to eat while outside. Of course it makes sense to ensure before the puppy arrives that your garden is securely fenced and all holes are blocked up, because if there is one, the dog will find it!

If you do not have a garden, or it is not convenient to take the puppy out frequently, you may decide to 'paper-train' him. Puppies prefer to urinate on an absorbent sur

face and will naturally go out of their way to use newspaper (or a rug!). You can make use of this instinct by gradually reducing the floor area covered with paper until only the area by the door is covered. Once the puppy is using the paper only in a small area, it is a simple step to move the paper outside the door.

Another point worth mentioning is the use of words when house-training. It is very useful to have a dog which will urinate on command. If you use the same words each time you take the puppy out he will soon associate the word with the required action. It does not matter what word you use but you should use one which will not cause embarrassment in public! 'Busy' or 'be quick' or 'hurry up' are popular.

Occasionally, a puppy will eat its own faeces and new owners are always very worried by this in case it means that the puppy has a nutritional deficiency. In most cases, however, it is just a habit, which started when the puppy was with its littermates, more out of curiosity than hunger. It is an unpleasant habit and the only way to stop it is to be very vigilant and remove all motions as soon as they are passed.

We have assumed so far in this chapter that the puppy is to live in the house. However some owners prefer to keep a dog in a kennel outside, or for him to sleep outside and come into the house during the day. It is possible to purchase custom-built wooden kennels with and without wire mesh runs attached, but any warm, draught-free place in an outbuilding, with bedding of blankets or straw, will serve as a kennel. If the dog is expected to pass urine and faeces in the run, it is better to have a concrete floor laid so that it can be kept clean and disinfected. The only alternative is to take the dog out frequently, but of course if he comes into the house at all, he should still be house-trained. Unless he is with other dogs, a puppy living outside will be very lonely and in winter an extra heat source will be required.

Indoor kennels are now gaining in popularity, and although they are quite expensive, they may save you a great deal of money as the puppy grows, if he has a tendency to be destructive. An indoor kennel is usually made of thick wire mesh and may be collapsible so that it can be stored when not in use and carried easily from place to place. They are available in all sizes to suit every breed. It is wise to introduce your puppy to one of these as early as possible, with a comfortable blanket and familiar toys. Once he will go into it willingly, you can try shutting the door for a few minutes. If the puppy does not seem too upset, the next stage is to gradually increase the time he is shut in until he will lie in the bed quietly on his own. It would not be fair to leave the dog shut in for hours on end but you should eventually be able to go out for a couple of hours knowing that he cannot get up to mischief.

GROOMING

Short-coated puppies will not need much coat attention other than a rub with a damp towel when they are dirty or a 'once-over' with a soft brush. However, they still need the discipline of being held and examined, and it is good practice to teach all puppies to have their mouths opened. If the dog will submit to this readily, it may save him suffering should he ever have a bone or other foreign body stuck in its mouth or throat, because you will be able to remove the obstruction quickly. Some breeds have a tendency to watery eyes, and your dog should let you wipe any discharge away with a piece of damp cotton wool. At this age the ears should be clean if they are healthy. If his nails are very sharp, it would do no harm to snip off the very tips with scissors or nail clippers, though you may prefer your vet to do it for you.

Long-coated puppies must be groomed from day one. It may be tempting to leave it a little while but this is a mistake – it will never be any easier. Initially all you need is a little stiff-bristled brush but after a few days you should attempt to use a wide-toothed comb. Your initial grooming attempts will influence your dog's attitude to grooming for the rest of its life, therefore you must try to make it pleasant for the puppy without giving in to him if he struggles. The best way is a little at a time with a titbit and plenty of praise afterwards.

The techniques of grooming a long-coated breed should have been demonstrated to you by the breeder. Otherwise, sit the puppy on your lap in a comfortable position, using one hand to hold the brush or comb and your other hand round the pup's body, holding the coat forward. Gradually tease the coat away from the holding hand, using the brush or comb, so that you have a parting, through which you can see the skin. Do a small section of the body at a time, adjusting the puppy's position on your lap as necessary. He should soon learn to lie still, even on his back, and most puppies seem to enjoy it after a while.

It should not be necessary to bathe a young puppy – the coat will be dirty from newsprint anyway – but if he becomes really filthy or is covered in parasites you may have to do so. It is very important to rinse and dry the dog thoroughly and to avoid shampoo or water entering his eyes and ears.

EARLY VISITS TO THE VET

Several references have already been made to visiting your vet, but you may not have made contact with one yet. You can find out the names of local practices from your business telephone directory (yellow pages) or you may see an advertisement in your local newspaper – until recently, vets were not permitted to advertise their services but now advertising is allowed. However the best

▲ *Grooming a Poodle puppy. The owner is teasing the coat away from the holding hand, making a parting through which the skin can be seen.*

way is by personal recommendation from another dog-owner, who will be able to tell you about the facilities offered by the practice they visit.

The first step is to telephone the practice to see if an appointment is required. When you arrive it is best to leave the puppy in the car or to wait outside until you are about to be seen, because the vet's waiting room is an ideal place to pick up infection. Some practices now run 'puppy clinics', which is an excellent idea, since the risk of cross-infection is minimised.

THE HEALTH CHECK

When you see the vet, the first thing he or she will do is to carry out a clinical examination to see if the puppy is healthy. He or she will take the puppy's temperature, examine his eyes for inflammation or defects, his ears for discharge, his mouth and teeth for poor conformation, his coat for parasites and listen to his heart and lungs, in order to detect any abnormal sounds which may suggest the presence of a heart defect. Before the examination is

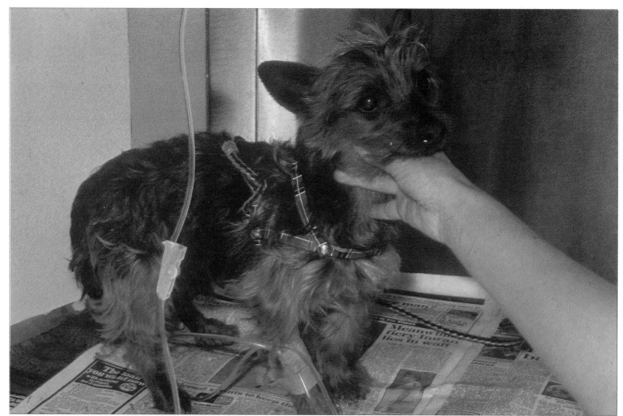

▲ *The intestinal form of parvovirus, like the other infectious diseases, may cause severe dehydration due to persistent vomiting and diarrhoea. To replace the fluid an intravenous drip is required.*

▲ *A careful veterinary examination is essential prior to vaccinating a young puppy.*

over you should take the opportunity to mention any problems which you have noticed such as sickness or diarrhoea, scratching, limping, etc. If the puppy seems healthy, you can then go on to discuss the diet and the important issues of vaccination and parasite control.

If a problem is found which the breeder did not mention, you have to make a difficult decision. You may be very fond of the puppy already, but if the vet thinks that the problem is serious, it is very advisable to return the puppy to the breeder with a certificate from the vet, giving the reasons. Provided this is done quickly your money should be returned or a replacement puppy offered. Minor defects, such as an overshot jaw, where the upper jaw is longer than the lower one, may not affect the dog's health but will render it useless as a show dog. Severe parasitic infestations can be treated if you wish but the breeder should be informed. Your vet will advise you.

VACCINATION

Puppies are usually vaccinated against four major infectious diseases.

■ **CANINE DISTEMPER.** This disease is still widespread in urban areas and areas where a low percentage of dogs are vaccinated. It is often fatal, and distressing as the course of the disease is long and relapses are common. Symptoms are vomiting, diarrhoea, high temperature, coughing and, later, fits, paralysis and twitching. Often there is thickening and peeling of the nose and foot pads which gave the disease its old name of 'hard pad'. Dogs which do recover are often left with permanent nervous system damage.

■ **INFECTIOUS CANINE HEPATITIS.** This disease is not encountered very often now in its severest form but if a dog does contract it, it may be fatal. Symptoms are high temperature, severe vomiting and dehydration, black diarrhoea and abdominal pain. If the dog survives it may develop a temporary opacity of the eye – this is known as 'blue eye'.

■ **LEPTOSPIROSIS.** There are two types of this bacterium which can cause disease in dogs. The more common type causes a high temperature, vomiting, very severe kidney damage and in fatal cases rapid kidney failure. The rarer type causes liver damage and jaundice and is transmissible to humans. This type of leptospirosis is transmitted by rats.

■ **PARVOVIRUS.** In 1978 a new disease of dogs was reported almost simultaneously in Great Britain, North America and Australia. In young puppies it caused heart failure and in older puppies and adults it caused severe vomiting, dehydration and bloody diarrhoea. The death rate was very high indeed. The virus was found to be similar to that which causes the most severe infectious disease of cats, and many people believe that the dog virus was a mutation of this cat virus. As most adult dogs are now immune, very young puppies nearly all have some protection from their mothers, therefore the heart type of parvovirus infection no longer occurs, but the intestinal form waxes and wanes continually in different parts of the country.

Combined vaccines against all these diseases, and also against some respiratory infections, are now available. However it is very important that the puppy is healthy and that the vaccines are administered at the correct time for maximum immune response. The protection which the puppy receives from its mother's milk may interfere with the vaccine and therefore the final dose must be given when this has disappeared, which in most puppies is just after 12 weeks of age. Two doses are required against leptospirosis, at least two weeks apart. You must then wait another two weeks after the final dose before it is safe to take the puppy out for walks where other dogs have been. The correct time for vaccination is very hard to predict, especially with parvovirus, but your vet will advise you when to bring the puppy, depending on the type of vaccine used and the degree of risk in your area. The final dose for parvovirus may be as late as 18 weeks.

PARASITE CONTROL

Puppies may be infected with both intestinal and external parasites.

■ **INTERNAL PARASITES.** Roundworms are found in virtually all puppies. The larvae migrate into the puppies' bodies from the mother's tissues before birth and they may also be ingested in the milk. Two species of roundworm are found in dogs, *Toxocara canis* and *Toxascaris leonina*. Mature worms will be present in the intestine of a puppy as young as two or three weeks of age and worms will continue to develop until six months when the puppy tends to become immune and will expel most of them naturally. Heavily infested puppies grow poorly, suffer from sickness, diarrhoea and bloating after eating. The larvae migrate through the lungs, possibly causing a cough and masses of worms eggs are found in the faeces. If young children handle puppies, they may themselves become infected, not with adult worms because they do not develop to maturity in humans, but with the larvae, which have been known to cause brain and eye damage. It is only *Toxocara canis* larvae which cause these problems but this is the more common parasite. However prevention of disease in children and puppies is easy by administration of anti-parasitic medication, which your

CARING FOR YOUR PUPPY

LIFE CYCLE OF THE ROUNDWORM

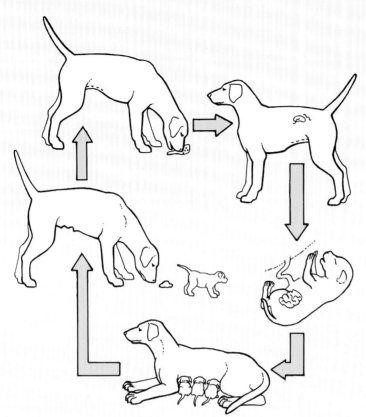

The embryonated infective eggs or larvae of the dog roundworm, *Toxocara canis*, are ingested by the dog (**1**) and migrate to the body tissues (**2**) such as the kidneys. Unfortunately, the larvae usually enter the tissues of developing foetuses (**3**) and localize in their intestines, being activated by pregnancy. After the birth of the puppies the larvae can also migrate into the puppies' system and infect them through the mother's milk (**4**). The worms mature, passing eggs in the puppies' faeces which are consumed by the mother and can reinfect her (**5**). Alternatively, larvae which fail to establish themselves and are passed out in the faeces may find another host and begin producing eggs. The eggs are not immediately infective, but need a short period outside the body to mature.

vet will supply. Worming should have been carried out at least twice by a responsible breeder before you buy the puppy but those from pet shops or puppy dealers may be very heavily infested. Worming should be repeated at least once a month until six months of age and yearly thereafter. Make sure to ask your vet to demonstrate how to administer tablets and liquid medicine.

Other types of worms are found occasionally in puppies usually when diarrhoea or anaemia is being investigated, such as hookworms or whipworms. Special medication for these may be required.

■ **EXTERNAL PARASITES.** Fleas and lice are the most usual parasites found in the coats of puppies. Fleas are brown or black in colour and move rapidly through the coat when the hair is parted. Even if you do not see the fleas themselves, you should see tiny black comma-shaped deposits in the coat. This is flea dirt and it is proof that fleas are present. Fleas only spend part of their time on the dog sucking blood and they may also hop on to cats or humans. They lay their eggs off the animal in cracks in wood, etc, therefore if reinfestation occurs, it is important to treat the house or kennel as well as the dog and also any other animals living in the house. Bedding should be washed and carpets vacuumed frequently.

In contrast, lice live wholly on the dog. They are more difficult to find as they do not move and are buried in the coat. They are grey in colour and tend to congregate round the head and ears. Dog lice only infest dogs and do not transfer to humans, therefore treating the dog alone is usually adequate. However, several treatments may be required as eggs will hatch out later.

Ear mites may also infest puppies, especially if they have been reared around cats, which often harbour these parasites. They cause intense ear irritation and scratching and a black discharge may be present. Again several treatments may be needed as the eggs will not be destroyed. Skin mites (mange mites) may be found in puppies, producing bald areas especially on the head and legs. Sarcoptic mange mites produce intense itching and are transmissible to humans.

Your vet will diagnose these problems and advise you on treatment, supply the necessary sprays, baths and so on. Be sure to follow the instructions carefully.

CHAPTER FOUR

The Growing Dog

*At 12 weeks this Samoyed puppy is still a bundle
of fluff, but between now and six months he will
outgrow his coat.*

▲ *Two American Cocker Spaniels enjoying a game of tug of war.*

BY 12 WEEKS OF AGE, your puppy should be growing steadily and will be beginning to lose the appealing 'bundle of fluff' appearance, as his legs and ears grow longer and he outgrows the puppy coat. In those breeds which have prick ears most puppies' ears are floppy at six to eight weeks but by 12 weeks a gradual lift should be noticed. If the ears have not lifted, they may not become fully erect until after six months but in a very few cases they fail to do so and that puppy will have so-called 'soft ears', which are undesirable for the show ring. Occasionally ears become pricked in breeds which are supposed to have folded ears, e.g., in Rough Collies. Breeders adopt various methods for supporting soft ears but it is difficult to say whether these methods are successful – basically it is a genetic problem. The puppy will also start to change his milk teeth for a permanent set, starting with the middle pair of small incisor teeth, top and bottom, at 12 weeks and finishing with the large canine teeth by six months. The toy breeds often have problems with tooth changing as the adult teeth may not push out the milk teeth, resulting in a double row or more often double canines. If the milk teeth have not been dislodged by eight months, they may be removed. In the male puppy the testes should have descended into the scrotum by six months and usually much earlier. If only one is present, by about one year, it is wise to have the dog castrated, or at least the retained testicle removed, as it may become cancerous in later life. Dogs with one testicle descended are called 'monorchid' and are usually unsuitable for showing.

FEEDING

By 12 weeks, your puppy will be eating more and will be able to tackle dog biscuits. Three meals a day are adequate at this age and it is usual to cut out one of the milky meals. Most dogs will reduce the number of meals by themselves. If the puppy is becoming choosy or fussy about food, provided he is otherwise healthy, it is a mistake to pander to the dog only feeding what it likes best or hand-feeding him. Puppies reared with other dogs rarely become fussy because of the element of competition but a puppy on his own may try to hold out for what he likes. This behaviour can be worrying but a dog will not starve itself. Sometimes a lump of something smelly, such as cat food, on top of his usual ration will start him off, and warming the food is helpful. If a meal is not eaten, leave it down for about 20 minutes and then remove it. Food fed straight from the refrigerator is rather unpalatable. If all food is refused for more than 24 hours you should ask your vet to examine the puppy.

Greedy puppies are easy to rear but at five or six months they may become very fat as their growth rate slows down. At this age, the number of meals should be reduced to two and the quantities reduced slightly.

THE GROWING DOG

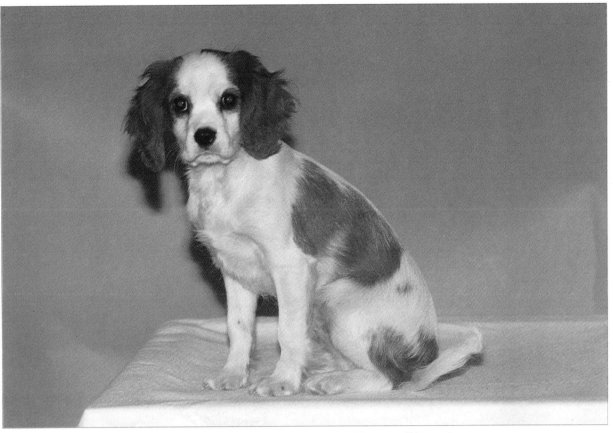

▲ *This Cavalier King Charles puppy is at the 'ugly' stage – all legs and ears.*

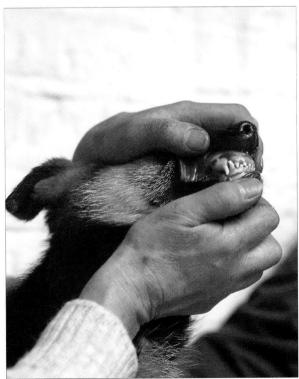

▲ *Permanent teeth will have replaced these milk teeth by six months of age.*

To be sure that the puppy is growing properly, you may wish to plot a growth chart. To weigh the puppy, first stand on the scales yourself, pick up the puppy and weigh both of you, and then subtract the two figures. You should have some idea from the breeder of what the eventual adult weight for that breed should be depending on whether it is a dog or a bitch. By 16 weeks, a dog should weigh approximately half its adult weight. Feeding giant breed puppies is a problem, and an art. If they eat adequate amounts of prepared puppy food, they should not require additional mineral or vitamin supplements. However at this age it is still possible for a large puppy to develop bone diseases, often manifest by deviation of the limbs from the perpendicular when viewed from in front or behind, simply because it is growing too fast. Breeders may help but many of them do overfeed their dogs, because they want to achieve maximum growth rate to obtain well-developed puppies and large, mature specimens for success in the show ring. If you have a giant breed puppy, you should consult your vet regularly about his dietary needs, because any bone problems must be corrected at the latest by six months so that permanent damage can be avoided. Puppies of the smaller breeds very rarely suffer from growth problems, and accuracy of dietary requirements is not nearly so important.

THE GROWING DOG

▲ *A grooming table, and an indoor kennel which can double as a carrying cage.*
◀ *A first visit to the grooming parlour. Poodles require regular clipping.*

GROOMING

Grooming of the long-coated breeds should become easier between three and six months as the fluffy puppy coat will be coming out and being replaced by adult coat. However as the puppy grows bigger and stronger, you will be unable to hold him on your lap and grooming must be carried out, either on the floor or, to avoid backache, on a table. A grooming table is a valuable investment for anyone with a large, long-coated dog – any table will do but it must be stable to give the dog confidence. Specially designed grooming tables are covered with rubber to prevent the dog from slipping, and some have wheels for transporting equipment at shows, which is very useful. At this age, a young dog may begin to rebel a little against being groomed – he must not be allowed to win, therefore it is advisable to enlist help to hold him if necessary. Be very firm and then praise him afterwards as before.

BASIC OBEDIENCE AT HOME

From a very early age, puppies recognize the meaning of a sharp tone of voice and a firm 'No!' if they are doing something naughty. As already stated under 'house-training', all training is based on praise for doing well rather than punishment, but if correction is required, it should be sharp and applied immediately the dog has done wrong, otherwise it is best forgotten.

The next thing a puppy learns is his name. A show dog may have a very long, complicated name but he must also have a short name which is easy for him to recognize. Use the name frequently and encourage him to come to you, especially when feeding him.

For the potential show dog which will be expected to attend shows soon after six months, show training should start almost as soon as you take him home. The most important lesson is to stand still in show position, head and tail up. If you have a small breed puppy, he must be accustomed to standing on a table to be examined by the judge. Large breed puppies may have to stand free, gaze up at their handler, or they may be positioned by the handler kneeling beside them. It is best to ask the breeder about this or visit a few shows to watch what other people do. Training to stand may be carried out just before a meal so that there is an immediate reward, and soon 'showing' for dinner can be replaced by 'showing' for a titbit.

Very soon, you should start putting a little collar on the dog. At first he will scratch at the collar and try to wriggle free, but as the dog learns that it will not come off, it will be accepted and forgotten about. The next stage is to attach a light leash or rope, preferably of material which cannot be chewed. Let the dog drag it about for a few minutes each day until it is ignored too. Then pick up the

▲ *A pup gets his first experience of discipline from his mother.*

leash and attempt to make the dog follow you, talking to him all the time. If there is a struggle, wait until the dog has stopped, then encourage him to come to you and give him praise.

Any puppy, whether destined for the show ring or not, should be taught certain basic obedience commands. One of the most important is 'COME' – no dog can be allowed off the leash when out at exercise unless the owner is confident that the dog will come when called, and there is nothing more infuriating than a dog which refuses to be caught. Many people with boisterous large breed dogs are afraid to let them off the leash at all and this is very sad for owner and dog. Training is best started in the garden, using a long leash. Retractable leashes ('flexi-leads') are now available which are very useful for this purpose, and for initial walks until the puppy is trained. The puppy should be given a considerable length of leash so that he is relatively free, then call his name and after that 'Come!' Repeating the command, pull him to-wards you and then give him praise. A titbit occasionally will be an encouragement, but you should expect your dog to come whether you have a titbit or not. It will not take many repetitions before the puppy realizes what is required and when he will do it off the leash you have won the battle. However there will be relapses, and the first time you let the dog off the leash out for a walk is very nerve-racking, but if the groundwork has been done you should not have too many problems. It makes sense

not to take your frustration out on a wayward puppy after you have eventually caught him – this will simply make him more determined not to come back next time! Going back to the leash work for a while longer should reinforce the training.

Another command often taught at an early age is 'SIT'. It is best not taught to show dogs unless you also teach them the meaning of 'STAND' – sitting in the show ring is undesirable. 'SIT' is an easy command to teach by putting pressure on the hindquarters while repeating the puppy's name and the command.

A more valuable lesson is 'LIE DOWN', or simply 'DOWN' (but remember not to use the same command to stop a dog from jumping upon people otherwise the dog will be confused). When the dog is in the sitting position gently pull out the front paws until he is forced to lie down, again repeating his name and the command, prais-ing him each time until he will do it on his own.

Walking to heel on the leash is very important and extremely difficult to teach, especially when there are so many exciting distractions out for a walk. Once again, therefore, heel-walking is best taught in the garden. At this stage, many people advocate the introduction of a choke-chain. The purpose of this is not to half-throttle the dog in the hope that it will teach him a lesson, because it probably will not. The choke-chain should be correctly fitted so that it will loosen as soon as tension is released; it should have large enough links that it does not catch on

▲ *Start training early — an obedient dog makes for a happier relationship between the two of you.*

the hair or cut into the skin, and it should be used in a series of sudden jerks followed by release rather than constant tension. If used in this manner, it also creates a jingling noise which adds to the effect. Each time the leash is jerked, the command 'HEEL' should be repeated, and if the dog insists on going in front of you, you may then correct this by changing direction repeating the 'HEEL' command. You should be firm about not allowing pulling from the beginning but if you are having trouble, training classes will be helpful, as described later.

There is one more important command for use inside

the house and that is 'BED'. Most outgoing puppies will enjoy meeting your friends and visitors but not all of them may like dogs. The puppy must be taught not to make a nuisance of himself, and to lie down when required. It is difficult to train a dog to 'GO AWAY', though some people do use this command. It is probably easier if he understands where you wish him to go and the most logical place is to bed. In addition he should be taught not to climb on the furniture or beds and it is wise still to restrict him to one room if possible, usually the kitchen, until you are certain that he is completely house-trained.

▲ *This car is fitted with a secure 'dog guard' to prevent the dogs jumping or being thrown into the front seats. However, a travelling crate would be more suitable for a small dog which could wriggle through the bars of a standard guard.*

◀ *Caught in the act!*

EXERCISE

First walks should be very short while the puppy is still growing. They should be aimed at showing him the big, wide world rather than tiring him out. He needs to be introduced to traffic and busy places, trains, buses and, of course, cars, to learn to be tied up outside shops and to meet strange people and other dogs. The distance covered may be increased very gradually so that it does not put too much strain on a puppy's still-growing bones and joints – a mile or so is plenty at this age.

TRAINING CLASSES

There are three kinds of training classes – those which cater to the potential show dog, which are called ringcraft classes, those which are for obedience, and those which prepare dogs for a newer type of canine activity, which is called agility. Agility competitions are a speed test incorporating jumps, tunnels, ramps, tables and other varied obstacles. They are great fun, but a young puppy is not physically developed enough to perform these exercises, therefore save this one until your dog is older. If you want help with training, ask around to find out where there is an obedience class for puppies and novices. On the other hand, if you are thinking of attending even one show, you must know what is involved, and your dog

must be accustomed to being handled by strangers and mixing with other dogs in close proximity. Attending ringcraft will prevent you both from making fools of yourselves and you can always switch to obedience later if you change your mind. Show dogs also have to walk properly on a leash, therefore both types of class will help you if you have a pulling problem. Training classes are not just for pedigree dogs – any dog will benefit from them and you will meet many interesting people.

TRAVELLING IN THE CAR

For most owners, especially those who have to take the dog to work, it is very important that the puppy should learn to be a good traveller.

The first few journeys should be very short and devoted entirely to the puppy. It is helpful to have an assistant to look after the pup, in addition to the driver. The back seat, or the back of an estate car (station wagon) or van, should be covered with a protective plastic sheet with towels on top in case the puppy should be sick. Car sickness is very common in puppies and it is due as much to nervousness and fear as to the motion of the car. Therefore the best way to combat it is to take the puppy in the car as often as possible until he is accustomed to riding. If the construction of the car will allow it, it is very desirable to have a dog-guard fitted so that the puppy cannot jump

THE GROWING DOG

TRAINING YOUR PUPPY

▲ A long lead is invaluable for teaching the puppy to come when called. Retractable leads are available which will allow the puppy considerable freedom, but still give you control when needed. 'Come' is the most important command for your puppy to learn.

▶ For most dogs sitting on command is easily learned. However, sitting down in the show ring is frowned upon.

▶ Always praise your puppy when he has done well.

▶ Walking to heel is the next most important lesson if walks are to be pleasurable for both dog and owner. A sharp jerk on the collar or choke chain, accompanied by the command 'heel', is required.

▲ *Show training cannot start too young, especially for small breeds which are required to stand posed on tables.*

over to the front seat and distract you when you are driving. Some puppies become very excited and will jump about, barking and yelping. This must not be tolerated because it makes driving difficult and possibly dangerous. The assistant should be able to stop this but sooner or later you may find that you have to take the puppy on your own in the car. The simplest way of solving this problem is to attach a fine rope to its collar and run the rope through the armrest on the back door back to your hand. At the first sign of noisy behaviour you can give the dog a jerk on its collar and say 'No!' very firmly. Remember to praise him when quiet. For very boisterous puppies which will not sit still, or for those with a tendency to chew the car, the best though expensive preven-

tion is to buy a travelling crate, similar in construction to an indoor kennel. These come in various shapes and sizes to suit most makes of estate cars (station wagons), vans or hatchbacks. Tiny puppies are probably better off in a travelling box in any case, as they may be thrown about and injured. These boxes have carrying handles and are invaluable for going to shows. They can of course be used in the house as well.

Most dogs love travelling once used to it and will curl up and go to sleep on a long journey. However if travel sickness is a persistent problem, your vet may supply you with tranquillizers for a long journey. Human travel sickness remedies are not very effective in dogs, except those containing chlorbutol which are certainly worth a try.

Consult your vet or give a child's dose 20 minutes before travelling.

THE FIRST SEASON AND NEUTERING

Bitches come into season (heat, or oestrus) for the first time any time from about five months to 15 months and very occasionally earlier or later than this. The usual time is between six and nine months. Many young bitch puppies have a slight yellow or greenish discharge before the first season. This should not cause concern as it will disappear afterwards.

The earliest sign is slight swelling of the vulva and a bloody discharge. If the bitch is very clean all that you may notice is increased licking but the discharge may be detected by dabbing with toilet paper. The red discharge will continue for about 10 days and will then become pink or clear. The vulva will be very swollen and then appear to slacken. The bitch will be very attractive to male dogs. Do not think that she is finished when the discharge changes colour – this is in fact the optimum time for mating. After another four or five days the pink or clear discharge gradually decreases, the vulva shrinks and the season is finally over about three weeks from the day the red discharge was first noticed. It has been known for bitches mated near the end of the season to become pregnant, therefore it is wise to be very vigilant during the whole three-week period. If unfortunately she is mated, you should consult your vet within 48 hours, as an injection can be given to prevent conception. However this will prolong the season, therefore you will have to be careful for an extra week at least.

▲ *Training is vital to teach a young dog obedience to simple commands, but allow him plenty of playtime too.*

After the season is over, for about eight weeks, a bitch which has not been mated will have a period of false pregnancy. She may show no signs at all or she may become quite mopey and produce milk. This is perfectly normal and treatment is unnecessary. Suddenly one day she will forget all about it and will be back to normal.

If you wish to have the bitch neutered (spayed), the safest times are either before the first season or three months after, when the normal period of false pregnancy is over. There is much controversy among vets about spaying bitches before the first season. Many believe that it causes problems in later life, such as urinary incontinence. However the operation itself is much simpler in immature bitches.

The procedure involves removing the womb and ovaries completely – it is in medical terms an ovarohysterectomy and it is a major abdominal operation. Nevertheless, most bitches recover extremely quickly and have to be restrained from running about, galloping up and down stairs, and so on, until the stitches are removed at 10 days. There are risks involved – from the general anaesthetic, bleeding and so on, although these problems are rare. You should discuss the matter thoroughly with your vet. Apart from saving the inconvenience of seasons, spaying young will protect the bitch from reproductive diseases and some types of cancer in later life. However many spayed bitches have a tendency to put on weight and if this is allowed to happen, it becomes very difficult to restore her figure without drastic dieting, so her diet must be watched as soon as she has recovered.

CASTRATION OF THE MALE DOG

This is a much simpler operation than spaying a bitch, with less risk involved, although a general anaesthetic is still required. Like spayed bitches, many castrated dogs have a weight problem and their diet must be carefully watched. Sometimes castrated males become very lethargic, therefore most vets advise leaving the operation until the dog is sexually mature. The quietening effect may be advantageous in the case of the very boisterous large breed male.

Hormone treatment is available for both dogs and bitches. In dogs the effect is similar to temporary castration and it may be worth trying if you are unsure whether or not to have the operation performed. If your bitch is due to come into season when you are on holiday or at Christmas or some other unsuitable time, you can ask your vet to give her an injection or tablets to abolish the signs until it is more convenient. With regular treatments you can prevent seasons altogether, although it makes more sense to have the bitch spayed. Breeders are suspicious of using these drugs in bitches which are intended for breeding later. The manufacturers say that there is no long-term effect on fertility but changes in the uterus have been reported, especially with the tablet form.

DOG BEHAVIOUR – AVOIDING COMMON PROBLEMS

All dog behaviour is controlled by the unwritten laws of the pack – some dogs are naturally dominant and others are submissive.

The submissive dog is easy to train. You are the 'pack leader' and the dog will be anxious to please you. Very submissive dogs are often nervous and may bite from fear. They will roll over on their backs, and even urinate, when chastised, just as they would do to indicate their submission to a dominant dog. The facial expression is ingratiating with ears laid back and head low. In a group of dogs this one will be pushed away from food and 'picked on' by the more dominant ones. Owners have a natural tendency to feel sorry for the submissive 'underdog' and to try to improve his lot by giving him more attention and protecting him. In most cases this makes matters worse because the dominant dogs will increase their efforts to put the submissive one 'in his place' and fights may ensue. The correct way to handle the situation is to feed the dogs separately and to reinforce the position of the most dominant dog, however much you would prefer to do otherwise.

The dominant dog, especially if he is a male, may present you with more problems. If a young puppy shows signs of genuine aggression towards you or anyone else, turn him over on his back or pick him up by his scruff. However, puppies often growl and bite your sleeve or your shoelaces in play and may catch your finger by mistake – this is quite different and should not be punished. All will probably be well until he begins to reach sexual maturity and that is the time when he may try to dominate you. This manifests itself by refusing to obey commands, and growling, or even worse, when punishment is meted out. No insubordination should be tolerated – at first you may think it is funny and let the dog get away with it, but a nine-month-old Rottweiler who wants to be boss is no joke. You must be prepared to prevent it from happening at all costs and so must all the members of your family. It is quite common for a dog to obey the husband but growl at the wife when she is left to deal with the dog while the husband is at work. The threatening attitude of the dominant dog is easy to spot – erect carriage, ears forward, hackles raised and an intent expression. Most dogs will not meet the human gaze but sometimes staring at an aggressive dog will induce an attack.

As stated previously, punishment for any canine offence should be carried out immediately if it is to have any effect. It is much better if you can avoid a confrontation,

▲ *These bloodhound pups are having a mock battle, which is a game, but it also teaches them to relate to other dogs.*

and sometimes ignoring the dog altogether can be an effective form of punishment. Praise should be lavish when he has done well and a titbit may be given, although too many should be avoided. If you have to punish your dog, try not to lose your temper however aggravating the situation is, and it is best not to use a leash, or other object which the dog should associate with pleasure. A very severe form of punishment is to pick him up by the scruff and shake him – this is the way one dog will discipline another. Do not do this too often however. Many people indicate their displeasure by brandishing a rolled-up newspaper, which is usually very effective.

Above all, when training a dog, you should try to be consistent, otherwise the dog will become confused. The best example of a mistake in training is the dog which jumps up on his owner. When he was a little puppy and jumped up looking for attention, the owner probably patted it and made a fuss over him. When he is too big, the owner suddenly realizes that   has become a problem, with muddy feet, ripped stockings, and so on, and starts to punish him – no wonder the dog is confused! To make matters worse, when he jumps up on his owner's friends or even strangers, they will not punish him in

case the owner objects. The answer is always to bend down at the knees to the dog to pat him, right from the beginning. If he jumps up, push him down gently and say 'Down!' or 'No!' firmly, and caress him when he keeps all four feet on the ground. As a last resort, bringing your knee up to his chest is a more effective deterrent than pushing him away, and of course you should not hit him on the face.

Probably the most important quality you need to train a dog is patience. Your dog is not mentally deficient if he does not immediately understand what you are trying to teach him!

Very occasionally the unlucky owner may find himself or herself with a dog which is quite unsuitable temperamentally for the owner's situation. A genuinely vicious dog should be put to sleep if he has bitten someone seriously without provocation. Otherwise the only alternative is to rehome him if you can find someone who is prepared to give him a chance. Unfortunately sending a dog away to be trained does no good at all – he may behave perfectly for the trainer but will resume his old behaviour when he comes home to you. Do not be afraid to seek help, either from breeders or from your vet.

THE ADULT DOG

The Adult Dog

Few dogs will win fame and fortune for their owners like this beautiful Crufts-winning English Setter bitch, but your dog will amply reward your love and care in many other ways.

BODY LANGUAGE

A dog's stance and expression give clear indication of mood and intent. This dog (**left**) wants to play and indicates this by lowering his elbows to the ground in a posture often described as the 'play bow'. The cat, however, is not so sure, judging by his threatening posture, open mouth and 'bottle' brush tail!

These dogs (**right**) are threatening one another and may well go on to fight. They are probably of nearly equal dominance, as shown by the forward ear position.

MOST DOGS ARE PHYSICALLY MATURE at nine months, i.e., their bones stop growing. However it may be two years before dogs of the large breeds finish muscle development and achieve their most imposing appearance. By nine months, your puppy ought to be house-trained, chewing should be less of a problem, and other basic training should be reasonably well advanced. In other words, you should be able to enjoy owning your dog with a little less work and hassle.

FEEDING

The mature dog which is kept as a pet needs less food than a growing puppy, and, in those breeds which have a tendency to be greedy, you may need to restrict food to the basic ration and be very careful about titbits. Most dogs do well on one big meal per day, usually given in the early evening, but if yours seems very hungry a small additional snack at breakfast or lunch time may keep him satisfied.

As explained previously, there are many prepared foods for dogs on the market – canned, frozen, preserved, semi-moist and dry. Some of these may be used as complete foods, especially the dried foods which are usually mixtures of flaked maize and other grains, dried meat or soya protein, fish meal, meat and bone meal, dried milk and some fats or oils. Vitamins and minerals are added but may disappear on prolonged storage. These foods should be soaked in water or gravy before feeding. They are inexpensive for the large breeds and very suitable for

THE ADULT DOG

▲ *Chewing is much enjoyed by all dogs – large raw bones and hide chews are most suitable.*
▶ *Involving your children in the care of the family dog will help to make them aware of others' needs.*

some dogs which are prone to digestive upsets. If your dog has been reared on canned puppy food, he can change to adult canned food from about six months old. Canned dog foods are usually not intended as complete foods and need to be mixed with biscuits or other carbohydrate source such as rice, bread or potatoes.

If you feed your dog fresh meat, you will need to supply some additional calcium, even if it is only milk. Milk is a valuable food but some dogs cannot digest it.

Semi-moist foods are usually made from soya protein with added vitamins and minerals and come in packets equivalent to one can. They may be fed as complete foods or a reduced quantity mixed with biscuit. They are very useful on vacations as they are clean and preparation time is minimal.

Quantities of food required vary between individuals and, as stated previously, you will only learn how much to feed by trial and error. It is a good idea to weigh the dog regularly if possible, to see that he is neither gaining nor losing weight, though with the giant breeds you may have to resort to a public weighbridge (weight scale), or a farmer's weighing crate, rather than the bathroom scales!

In addition to their basic diet, many dogs enjoy hide chews and these will keep them occupied while being safer than bones. Any bones given should be large ones. Vegetables and fruit are also liked by plenty of dogs – carrots are a very useful replacement for biscuits if the dog tends to be overweight. The extra fibre in vegetables is beneficial but does tend to create wind for the first few days.

If you exercise your dog in fields or on bridle paths, you will probably notice that he has a liking for cow or horse dung. Although large amounts may make him sick, this is natural behaviour – when a carnivore kills a graz-

THE ADULT DOG

▲ *Regular clipping is necessary for breeds, such as the Poodle, which do not shed their coats.*

▶ *The long feathers on the tail and legs of the Irish Setter are prone to tangling. They should be brushed out regularly.*

ing animal, one of the first parts of the body that he will eat is the intestines, a valuable source of vitamins. Similarly, dogs like to chew horn trimmed from horses' feet by the blacksmith. However you should beware of the cows' hooves which are sold as toys for dogs – they have been known to cause intestinal obstruction if swallowed whole.

GROOMING

By nine months, dogs of the long-coated breeds have usually acquired a beautiful profuse coat. If you are interested in showing, this is the time for your dog to make his debut in the puppy classes. Once he is over a year old he will probably lose it all again and look terrible for several months. Breeds with double coats lose the soft undercoat once or twice a year but seldom lose the top coat. Therefore, during a period of moulting, the loose undercoat should be combed out, using a blunt-toothed metal comb. Varying widths between the teeth are available for different parts of the body – narrow for the legs and head and wide for the tail, trousers and ruff. You should work right down to the skin systematically over the whole body to prevent matting. Brushing over the surface is not enough. Male dogs tend to lose coat according to the weather, whereas bitches' coats are under hormonal influence and tend to be lost about three months after

THE ADULT DOG

▲ *Some breeds are prone to running eyes causing brown marks on a light-coloured coat. Ask your vet to check your dog's eyes if you notice a permanent discharge, and keep the area clean with frequent bathing.*

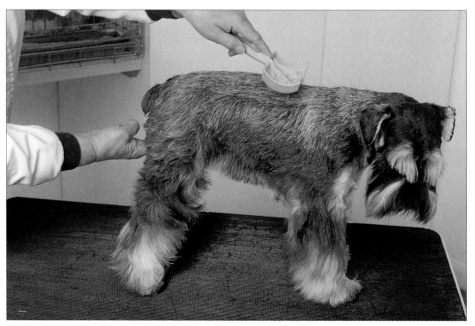

▲ *Dogs with a natural short coat or one that has been trimmed can be kept adequately groomed with a stiff brush.*

▲ *A Samoyed bitch in full coat, about six months after whelping.*

▲ *The same bitch about 3 months after whelping.*

oestrus. A bitch will usually lose almost all her coat three months after having puppies and will probably not be in show condition again until about six months after whelping. Other long-coated dogs such as Old English Sheepdogs or Afghans and of course the Poodles, Spaniels and Terriers, if they are not to be shown, will be much more comfortable and easy to keep if the coat is clipped short. Badly matted dogs often have to be groomed by a professional under sedation, or even general anesthesia if very bad. Prevention is much easier and less expensive. Small areas of matted coat, such as are often found on the ears and feet or around the tail, may be snipped off with scissors, taking great care not to cut the skin.

Moulting in the short-coated breeds tends to be more spread out and often owners complain that hair falls out all the time. This is quite natural but may be accentuated in well-heated houses. A daily brushing with a soft brush will help to remove loose hairs. Regular bathing is not necessary for dogs except for show purposes (see 'Showing'), to make them more pleasant to live with and to treat certain skin conditions.

▶ *More advanced training – this obedient dog has retrieved a dumbell and brought it back to his handler.*

Instead of discarding moulted undercoat, you could spin it like sheep wool and use it to knit garments – they are very soft and feel like Angora. Samoyed or Pyrenean wool, being white, can be dyed to a variety of colours. Body wool is best for this purpose and you should discard wool from the legs, trousers and tail. If you do not wish to take up spinning yourself, there are plenty of dog owners who have done so and may be prepared to do it for you for a small fee.

EXERCISE

Your dog will now be going out for regular walks once or twice a day. For many people this is the most enjoyable aspect of dog owning, therefore it is a pity if you allow your dog's behaviour to spoil it for you by not coming when called, jumping up on strangers or pulling on the leash. Teaching a dog to walk properly on a leash is not easy and you should not give up. If all else fails and you cannot control him on a collar or choke chain, a kind of head-collar is available similar to that used on horses. Once you have control of his head you need not fear that

he will pull you over, no matter how big he is. Your dog will not like this piece of equipment to begin with and will try to remove it, but will eventually become accustomed to it. For the dog which will not come when called, despite rigorous training efforts, or has to be walked where there are farm animals, a retractable leash is invaluable, allowing the dog some freedom without the risk of losing him altogether. It is almost impossible to teach a dog not to chase farm stock, cats, rabbits and other small animals, unless he has been brought up with them, and it is safer not to allow him the opportunity. Any farmer has the right to shoot a dog which he or she considers is a danger to his or her livestock, and most will do so without hesitation. The damage to sheep every year, especially pregnant ewes or those with lambs, is horrific. However, if you do have access to an aggressive ram, it is said that a short time confined with him in a pen will make the most confirmed sheep-chasing dog think again! Even young sheepdogs have to be trained and they learn by copying older dogs, being sternly reprimanded if they show any sign of wanting to chase or bite.

It is most important that all dog owners should be very

▲ *Choke chains are a useful training aid, but they must be fitted correctly. Small link chains should not be used on long-coated dogs as they become entangled with the hair.*

▲ *Fitted properly, a choke chain should loosen immediately once the lead is slackened.*

▲ *An agility competition – enjoyed by dogs as much as humans.*
◄ *The working gundog – a Labrador Retriever in action.*

vigilant about where they allow their dogs to defaecate. Dog mess on pavements and in parks has caused a great deal of anti-dog feeling. Ideally your dog should only pass a motion in your garden and if he does so elsewhere you should be prepared to clean up after it.

The distance which you go on walks will depend on your enthusiasm more than the dog's, but you should remember that any animal has to be fit to go for long distances, therefore it is unfair to expect him to go 20 miles once a month if the normal daily walk is two miles. Puppies of the large breeds less than nine months should also be gradually introduced to prolonged exercise. Some individuals in any breed are naturally lazier than others, but if your dog finds difficulty with exercise, he should be examined by your vet, especially if there is marked breathlessness or lameness after a rest.

FURTHER TRAINING

Your young dog should be able to proceed to more advanced training and work after he is a year old. If he is a gundog, he should be introduced to specialized training, preferably along with older experienced dogs. Books are available on the subject of gundog training. The dog should fetch and carry objects naturally but you will need to teach him to find a dummy in long grass or undergrowth and to bring it back to you reliably, giving it up when asked to do so instead of playing with it.

Field trials are competitive events which test the gundog's working ability without actually shooting. A show gundog cannot become a full champion without competing in these events. Most gundogs work two or three days per week during the shooting season and as they will cover long distances during the day, they may need extra meals of concentrated nutritious food on the days when they are not working. However the total quantity fed will probably be no more than one and a half times their normal requirement.

If you wish to do agility or obedience work with your dog it is best to attend classes, but remember that you will need to practise what you have learned every day. Obedience work requires tremendous discipline as competitions are won or lost on the accuracy of a required movement and only a few points separate the winner from the also-ran. In agility classes, the dog is expected to complete a course of obstacles – jumping over fences without knocking them down, weaving through a line of upright poles, diving through a tunnel of material when he cannot see the other end, negotiating a see-saw and staying on a tabletop for five seconds or so. The winner is the dog with the fastest time and the fewest mistakes. The handler runs with the dog, directing and encouraging him. Most of the canine competitors seem to enjoy the event greatly once they understand what is required of them,

THE ADULT DOG

▲ *Dog training classes can be great fun and offer invaluable advice and support.*

▶ *Labrador Retrievers love water and fording a river is all in a day's work.*

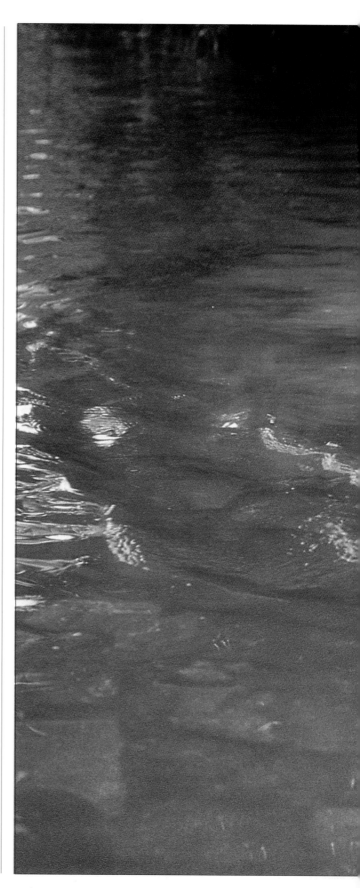

but the difficulty is for the handler to insist on accuracy without losing speed.

The show dog requires the least training – all he has to do is to stand still to be examined by the judge and to trot round the ring without pulling on the leash or getting mixed up with the other dogs. However the dog must have patience, a steady temperament and sufficient personality and stamina to show himself off throughout the day without becoming tired or jaded. That essential sparkle cannot be created by training – a show dog is born, not made.

VACATION TIME

The sight of suitcases upsets most dogs and leaving your pet behind when you go on holiday is quite a wrench for the owner too. If you cannot leave him with friends or relatives, you will be forced to leave him in boarding kennels or to take him with you. Although you can take a dog to most countries with you, provided the important requirements of the country you are visiting are met, you cannot take a dog into the United Kingdom without him spending six months in a quarantine kennel. There are no exemptions from this rule. The reason is, of course, prevention of the dreaded virus disease rabies, which is transmissible to humans and which is always fatal.

It is quite possible to find hotels and guesthouses

THE ADULT DOG

▲ *Kennels usually have an indoor sleeping area, which is heated, and outdoor runs.*

where the proprietors will accept well-behaved dogs. However your dog will not be accepted in the dining room and not usually in any of the public rooms, therefore it becomes very difficult unless you are travelling by car and can leave the dog in it while you are having your meals. Very quiet dogs may be left in hotel bedrooms but proprietors are understandably wary about dogs curling up on the beds, urinating on the carpets, or worse, and attacking any hotel staff. Many hotels and guesthouses no longer accept dogs because of previous bad experiences and therefore it is most important that your room should be left as you found it. It also helps to foster goodwill if you take food with you for the dog and enquire whether it is suitable to exercise the dog, rather than just letting him loose on the lawn.

If you are travelling by bus or train, you can make your dog feel more at home by taking a blanket for him, some water in a bottle, a bowl and a few biscuits. You should do your utmost to avoid the dog being a nuisance to other passengers and it is always wise to ask nearby passengers if they object – after all they may be allergic to dogs. On trains, dogs should really travel in the guard's van or baggage car, although usually no one minds when they are with you in the carriages, provided they do not cause problems. You should never allow the dog on the seats – small dogs are better kept in travelling boxes.

▲ *Two dogs from the same household will be happier sharing a kennel while you are away.*

▲ *If you* must *leave your dog in the car, park in a shaded area, open the windows slightly and leave a bowl of water. Never leave your dog for any length of time.*

BOARDING KENNELS

Finding a good boarding kennel is not always easy. Personal recommendation being the best way, and the really good ones are always busy at peak holiday periods, therefore you have to make your reservation well in advance. It is wise to start leaving your dog in a kennel when he is quite young as he will settle in more quickly. Older dogs left in kennels for the first time may not eat much and may lose a great deal of weight through fretting. Of course, kennel owners are used to dealing with these problems. If your dog has a medical complaint, you should discuss the problem with the kennel staff and if necessary arrange for a vet to examine the dog when you are away, or to supply medication. All boarding kennels will insist on an up-to-date vaccination certificate against the four major diseases and also probably against 'kennel cough'. This respiratory infection acquired its name because it can spread rapidly through a group of dogs – it is very contagious and if one visiting dog has it, it may ruin that kennel's business for the whole summer holiday period. The vaccine is administered up the nose instead of by injection. It is not completely foolproof but should lessen the severity of an attack, even if it is not prevented. When you are choosing a kennel, it is wise to visit several so that you can make comparisons. Flashy facilities are not very important – what matters is the way the dogs are cared for, how they are exercised, fed and watered, and general hygiene.

DOGS IN CARS

Whether you are travelling on holiday or keeping your dog in the car at work, one of the dog owner's most worrying problems is how to keep the dog cool when you have to park in the sun. Keeping him warm in the winter is simple – just provide more blankets – but the summer sun can be a killer. The temperature inside a car, even with the windows half-open, can rise rapidly to well over 100°F (38°C). The problem may be solved by parking in the shade, if you can find any, but remember that the earth moves relative to the sun and if you leave the dog for several hours you may return to find that the car is no longer in the shade. You can purchase reflective car covers, but if you have to leave your dog, one of the best ways of keeping the car cool is to cover it completely with sheets or towels and soak them in water – the evaporation keeps the temperature down. Of course you will have to add water periodically as they dry out. It is amazing that owners do not recognize how dangerously like an oven a car can become – some people even leave babies in them.

BREEDING A LITTER

CHAPTER SIX

Breeding a Litter

*When you have a much-loved pet, it is always
tempting to breed from her or him.*

TO BREED OR NOT TO BREED

People breed dogs for a variety of reasons, some more valid than others. Here are a few examples.

▌ 'TO IMPROVE THE BREED BECAUSE MY DOG/BITCH HAS AN EXCEPTIONAL TEMPERAMENT/WORKING ABILITY/CONFORMATION/COLOUR ETC.'

These are very good reasons providing one is not perpetuating any feature which is extreme, and which in other breeds would be considered an unsoundness. You should remember also that heredity is a complicated business and the puppies may be disappointing.

▌ 'TO MAKE MONEY.'

Commercial dog breeders do make money out of breeding – they would not do it otherwise. However, dog breeding will not make you wealthy, as the cost of rearing puppies is considerable. There will not be a great market for your puppies unless dogs of your breeding become well known in the show ring or in a performance field, and one cannot build up this kind of reputation overnight. Showing and advertising are additional costs to consider.

▌ 'TO KEEP A PUPPY, A SON/DAUGHTER OF MY MUCH-LOVED PET.'

This is fine, provided you remember that dogs usually have more than one puppy, and sometimes 10 or more. You will have to sell or find good homes for the rest, and it has been known for people to become so desperate, with a houseful of growing pups which they could not afford to keep, that they had to put the remaining pups to sleep. This is a heart-breaking experience.

▌ 'BECAUSE IT WILL DO THE BITCH GOOD.'

This is a very difficult point. There is probably a very slightly reduced incidence of mammary tumours in older bitches which have had a litter compared with those which have not, but it would be much better to have her spayed instead. The risk of womb infections in old age may also be slightly reduced but this is doubtful. A very fussy, thin bitch may eat better and put on weight after a litter. Otherwise it will make no difference to her at all.

▌ 'TO TEACH THE CHILDREN ABOUT REPRODUCTION.'

This might be more cheaply managed with a pet mouse or guinea pig, and is also a rather selfish reason. The important thing to avoid is deliberately bringing into the world animals which will end up unwanted and possibly mistreated. There are enough stray dogs in the world already.

HEALTH OF THE BITCH

The ideal age to breed from a bitch is at her second or third season. It is not a good idea to have a first litter if she is over the age of six years. Of course many vets will remember instances of 10-year-old bitches having first litters with no problems, but these are very few and far between. If a bitch is mated accidentally at her first season, it will probably do her no harm, but physically and mentally she is still immature.

The bitch should be in good but not fat body condition before mating. She should be vaccinated, wormed and checked for fleas and lice. If you are in doubt about any aspect of her health, your vet should examine her before mating and if she has any major problems you should question seriously your reasons for breeding from her. Apart from the stress of pregnancy and lactation which may be harmful for the bitch, certain diseases or defects may be inherited by the puppies. The way in which these problems are transmitted may be poorly understood but hip dysplasia, heart defects and epilepsy are examples of conditions which are suspected to be partly hereditary. Some diseases, such as a type of progressive blindness called retinal atrophy and the blood clotting disorder haemophilia, are known to be hereditary. If your bitch is of a breed which is known to suffer from a hereditary disease, she should be checked for that disease if possisble, e.g., by having her hips X-rayed or her eyes examined by a specialist. Your vet will then be able to advise you how to proceed. Hip dysplasia is a condition which causes lameness and difficulty in rising, climbing stairs and so on in severe cases. It is found in most of the large breeds of dog. In certain breeds, hip dysplasia may occur in almost every animal. In this situation, you cannot only breed from animals with normal hips because all the other good qualities of the breed would be lost, therefore it is important to know what the average standard of hips is for that breed. If the dog's hips are better than average it may be considered for breeding and if worse, it should be rejected. For this reason, there are official schemes in several countries for assessing X-rays and rewarding a score for hip status.

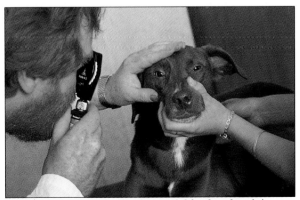

▲ *An eye examination is essential for those breeds in which inherited eye diseases, such as progressive retinal atrophy, hereditary cataract or Collie eye anomaly, occur.*

BREEDING A LITTER

HIP DYSPLASIA

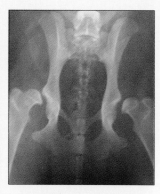

Hip dysplasia is a widespread problem in most of the large breeds. It is prevalent in the German Shepherd Dog where breeding for excessive hind-limb angulation may have contributed to the problem. The X-ray (**above**) shows a particularly severe case, where there is no contact between the pelvis and the head of the femur (thigh bone).

THE STUD DOG

The same health considerations apply to a prospective stud dog as to the bitch but they are even more important as the dog has the potential to produce many more puppies. However a successful stud dog must have qualities other than good health – he should have a good temperament, preferably he should be good-looking, or at least a good worker, he should be fertile and he should be keen to mate, even with difficult bitches. Surprisingly, many a breeder has planned a mating which she or he believed would produce a world beater, only to find that the dog and bitch would have nothing to do with each other!

There may be a very nice dog living down the road if you are extremely lucky, but generally you will have to be prepared to travel, sometimes long distances, to a suitable dog.

Dog breeders are usually very anxious about matching pedigrees and some show dogs are very inbred – the result of father/daughter or mother/son or half-brother/half-sister matings. This experiment can be successful if carried out by someone who knows the dogs and their background very well and who is aware of the risks of producing puppies with hereditary defects. However, close line-breeding is best avoided. Most show dogs have some names common to both sides of the pedigree but there is no point in deliberately mating your bitch to a dog descended from the same great champion unless you know that the good points of that dog are the ones that you wish to perpetuate. Remember that all dogs have faults, even the great ones, and by line-breeding to a particular dog you are 'doubling up' on his faults as well as his good points. The honest breeder will be pleased to advise you on the choice of a stud dog, but beware of the person who says, 'Well, there's always my dog ...' It is a mistake to assume that mating your bitch to the top-winning dog in the country will ensure that your puppies will also be successful. Often, the puppies look like neither parent, or stubbornly inherit the one fault which you were trying to breed out. However, in general, if you mate together a good bitch and a good dog, there will be at least one or two show quality specimens in the litter.

Traditionally the stud fee used to be the same as the price of a puppy, and some stud-dog owners would accept a puppy instead of a fee. You should ascertain before the mating whether you are expected to pay the fee whatever happens, or whether the stud-dog owner will allow a repeat mating free of charge if there are no puppies born. Ideally any financial arrangements should be written down, as they may be the subject of arguments later. If you are not prepared to allow the stud-dog owner 'pick of the litter' instead of a fee, this should also be sorted out before the mating. You may be able to reduce the fee by finding a lesser-known brother of a famous champion and using him instead. Whatever you decide you should make the arrangements well in advance – it is a mistake to assume that you will be allowed to bring your bitch to be mated at a moment's notice. Stud-dog owners may be very choosy about which bitches they will accept for their dog, and may ask to see her pedigree, hip X-rays and other data.

THE REPRODUCTIVE CYCLE

Bitches normally come into season every six months but the interval may be less or considerably more. Some breeds only have a season once a year. They may be irregular and this is not abnormal. The signs of oestrus were described in the chapter on the growing dog and the whole business lasts about three weeks. The optimum time for mating is usually about 10 to 12 days after the first sign of a bloody discharge, therefore it is important that the early signs are not missed. Some bitches may be ready for mating earlier or later than this and the best time is one or two days after she is prepared to stand for the dog to mate her. She will indicate her readiness for mating by holding her tail to one side and spreading her legs slightly in preparation for taking the dog's weight. If you cannot be sure which is the correct day, your vet may be able to help by performing a series of vaginal smear tests, as the cells lining the vagina change in appearance as the season progresses.

The gestation period (i.e., the time taken for the puppies to develop) is nine weeks. However anything from 60 to 66 days is not unusual and puppies may be born up to a week early or late. As stated previously, bitches which are not mated, or do not conceive, normally have a period of false pregnancy which is also about nine weeks.

Bitches will continue to come into season throughout their lives, although the signs may be less intense as they reach old age. They do not have a menopause like women.

MATING AND PREGNANCY

When you think that your bitch is ready for mating, it is usually best to take her to the stud dog rather than vice versa. Male dogs are often somewhat distracted if they are taken on to strange premises.

It is expecting a great deal of any bitch to be ready to mate without at least a short period of courtship. If possible either the bitch or the dog should have been mated before, as two inexperienced dogs may play around for ages and never actually get round to doing it! They should not be left along together for long in case the bitch attacks the dog – very rarely does the opposite happen and a young dog may be put off mating for life if he is injured by an aggressive bitch, which is not ready for his attentions. Inexperienced, nervous or aggressive bitches may have to be restrained quite firmly but there is no point in trying to hold a bitch which genuinely resents being

MATING

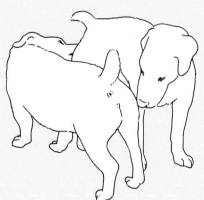

As a prelude, the dogs sniff each other's genital region (**left**) and after a variable length of courting, the bitch will allow the male to mount, standing with her tail aside.

A tie (**right**) is usually formed which lasts several minutes.

Finally, the dogs swivel round (**below**) and remain standing quietly facing away from each other, joined in the genital lock.

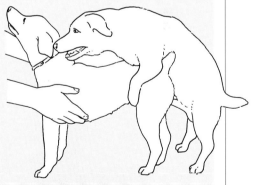

Mating in dogs is usually supervised, certainly at a stud. Some ailments can be transmitted by sexual contacts between dogs, notably the canine venereal tumour and brucellosis. Any signs of abnormal swelling, possibly indicative of a tumour, should be reported to a veterinarian without delay, and the dog should not be mated. Screening for brucellosis is possible.

▲ *A heavily pregnant Labrador bitch.*

THE WHELPING BOX

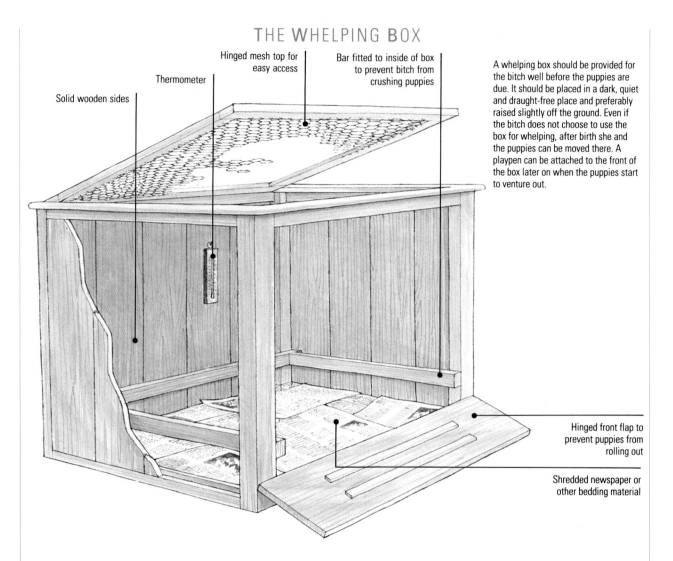

Solid wooden sides

Thermometer

Hinged mesh top for easy access

Bar fitted to inside of box to prevent bitch from crushing puppies

A whelping box should be provided for the bitch well before the puppies are due. It should be placed in a dark, quiet and draught-free place and preferably raised slightly off the ground. Even if the bitch does not choose to use the box for whelping, after birth she and the puppies can be moved there. A playpen can be attached to the front of the box later on when the puppies start to venture out.

Hinged front flap to prevent puppies from rolling out

Shredded newspaper or other bedding material

mated, as it probably means she is not ready. It is better to give up and try again the next day.

Mating in dogs takes quite a long time – up to 30 minutes or so. This is because of a peculiarity of anatomy of the dog's penis – a swelling two or three inches back from the tip, which is held by the bitch's vaginal muscles so that they cannot be separated. This is called 'the tie'. Dog breeders often attach great importance to the length of the tie, but in fact it matters little whether it lasts five minutes or 45 as far as the likelihood of conception is concerned. In fact it has been known for bitches to conceive even if no tie occurs. However, it is generally accepted that a proper mating has not taken place if no tie is achieved. The dogs may become restless during the tie and the male usually turns round so that he is standing tail to tail with the bitch. The tie will end by itself quite naturally and you should not attempt to separate the dogs forcibly. If your bitch has been mated by mistake and you find the dogs together, separating them would do not good – it would be too late.

One mating at the correct time is all that is necessary to produce puppies. However if a bitch has had difficulty conceiving, it may be advisable to mate her several times during the oestrus period, every day for two or three days or with a day between matings. You should not assume that the stud-dog owner will be prepared for this and it is best to arrange it beforehand.

Once she has been mated you will have to be patient for several weeks before you find out whether or not she is pregnant. A vet can usually diagnose pregnancy in a slim, relaxed bitch at three to four weeks by feeling her abdomen for a series of little golfball-sized swellings. If the vet cannot feel anything at this stage, it is best to wait until seven weeks when they will be easier to feel. If he or she is still unsure, the bitch may be X-rayed at this stage as the puppies' skeletons will have begun to form and are visible on X-ray film. By this time, the bitch will have a noticeably larger abdomen and her teats will be prominent and pink. Unfortunately, however, some false pregnancies can be very convincing, even to the false labour

THE BIRTH PROCESS

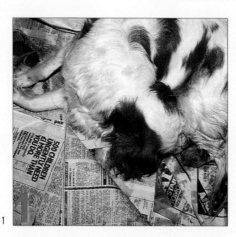

1 Puppies are often born tail first; in this case the puppy's emerging head is visible. The bitch breaks the 'water bag' with her teeth.

2 The puppy has now emerged fully but it still joined to the bitch by the umbilical cord.

3 The placenta is passed, usually after each puppy, and is eaten by the bitch. The dark-green coloration is normal. Here the umbilical cord is still intact, but the bitch will chew through it.

4 The newborn pup is licked by the mother until it is clean and dry. It quickly finds a teat and begins to suck. The first milk, or colostrum, is very important as it contains antibodies which pass into the newborn puppy's system.

▲ *Poodle puppies at 2 days old.*

pains! Even experienced dog breeders have been fooled.

Some bitches become very hungry during pregnancy, whereas others will be extremely fussy. Occasionally a bitch will develop a sort of craving for one particular food, almost like a woman. Therefore one cannot lay down hard and fast rules for feeding bitches during pregnancy. However, there is no requirement for extra food until after six weeks, and it is doubtful whether overweight bitches should be fed anything extra at all, except possibly additional vitamins and minerals. During the last three weeks of pregnancy the bitch should be given 50% more food than usual, but she may need several small meals, rather than one large one, as her stomach capacity will be smaller. She will refuse food immediately prior to whelping.

Near the end of pregnancy, the bitch will find exercise difficult. However it is important to keep her as fit as possible, so she should have plenty of exercise, preferably walking on a leash, during the first eight weeks. As whelping approaches, she will start looking for a place to have her puppies. You should decide quite early on where you wish her to whelp, ideally a secluded warm, dark place such as a large cupboard, or in the spare room, or in a shed, if it can be heated to provide the puppies with air temperature of over 80°F (27°C). When extra heating is required, especially in winter, the heat

source should be placed so that neither bitch nor puppies can burn themselves on it. A heat lamp such as is used for piglets is quite suitable. A kennelled bitch will be quite happy outside provided other dogs are kept away from her.

Most breeders using whelping boxes. You can buy them from dog equipment suppliers, and some are quite sophisticated with heated floors. However it is quite simple to make a suitable whelping box. Toy bitches may be quite happy with a strong cardboard box with one side partially cut away. Larger bitches will need a wooden box. For an average-sized bitch of about 50 lb (22.5 kg) a suitable size would be length 4 ft (120 cm), depth 3 ft (90 cm), height 2½ ft (76 cm). It is a good idea to have a low front to the box about 9 in (22.5 cm) high to prevent the pups from falling out, and to put an internal bar around the other three sides about 6 in (15 cm) from the base, so that a puppy trapped behind a bitch will not be squashed or suffocated.

When the box is finished you can cover the floor with several layers of newspapers and then place on top of these blankets or, ideally, the synthetic fleecy bedding material such as that used in hospitals. The bitch should find the bed quite attractive, although is she seems unimpressed you may have to persuade her to climb in. It is important to introduce her to the whelping box well in

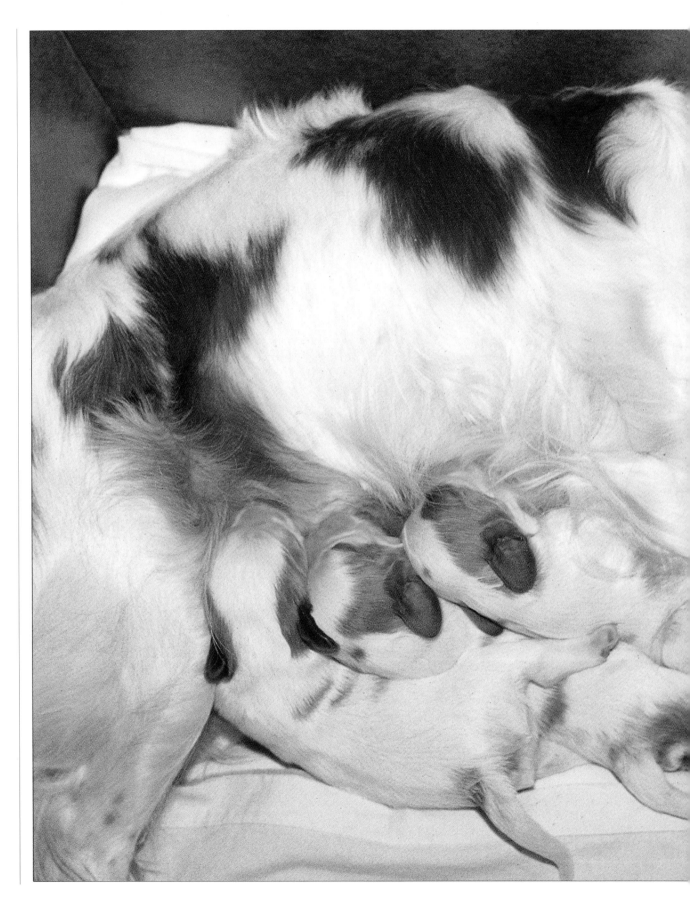

BREEDING A LITTER

advance, otherwise she may decide to have her puppies on your bed, or under a hedge in the garden.

THE BIRTH

Birth is divided into three stages. The first stage is when the puppies move towards the birth canal which gradually dilates so that they can be pushed along it. The second stage is the expulsion of the puppies to the outside and the third stage is when the afterbirths come away.

The first stage may last quite a long time, especially with first litters – up to 24 hours is quite common. The body temperature of the bitch is a good guide to imminent whelping. It drops by at least one degree and often more. It is taken by inserting a clinical thermometer, previously shaken down and lubricated with liquid paraffin or vaseline, into the rectum (back passage) for one minute. The normal temperature of a dog is 101.5°F (38.6°C) but many dogs are lower than this anyway and so you should repeat the procedure twice daily for several days before she is due. By doing this, you will know what your bitch's normal temperature is and you will recognize the fall when it occurs. At this stage, you should warn your vet so that he or she is prepared should assistance prove necessary.

The signs of first stage labour are food refusal, panting and bed-making. Presumably the bitch is feeling pains in her abdomen at this stage, and she may seem very anxious and restless. However no action is necessary unless the signs persist for more than 24 hours with no further action, at which stage she should be checked. She may simply be unhappy with something in her environment, usually too much disturbance, and if left alone will settle down.

At the onset of second stage labour, the bitch usually lies down and starts to use her abdomen muscles, i.e. straining. During these contractions, she will stop panting which makes them more obvious. From the beginning of straining a puppy should appear within a half hour. If it does not, veterinary assistance should be summoned. The usual reason for difficulty with a first puppy is that it is emerging backwards. This is not abnormal – 40% of puppies are born tail first. However the hind legs are the wrong shape to dilate the birth canal and therefore a first puppy coming backwards may get stuck. If you can see toes protruding from the vulva, it will do no harm to give them a gentle pull as the bitch strains, but unless you are experienced it is unwise to attempt any other interference. Once the first puppy has arrived the bitch should lick at it enthusiastically, and she will swallow the membranes and fluid. Sometimes a puppy will be born still inside its

◀ *A contented bitch with all her puppies sucking well.*

97

BREEDING A LITTER

▲ *Cavalier King Charles Spaniel pups at 8 weeks old.*

shiny envelope, and a novice bitch may not know what to do. In this case, you will have to break the bag yourself, otherwise the puppy will suffocate, and encourage her to lick it. This stimulates the puppy and starts it breathing. Very quickly it will be squirming around like a little blind rat looking for the milk supply. If the pup appears lifeless, try shaking it, head down, to encourage fluid to run out of its nose and mouth, and rub it very briskly with a towel. This usually starts breathing. Sometimes, of course, puppies are born dead, and there is nothing you can do, but they can survive a remarkably long time without breathing, therefore it is worth persevering as long as the heart is beating.

Once started, the bitch should produce puppies at roughly half-hour intervals. However, it is quite common for several pups to appear quickly and then none for a few hours, during which time the bitch will rest. It is a problem knowing when she has finished. Afterbirths may come after each pup, or several may come together. They are greenish-black in colour and it may be difficult to count them as the bitch will quickly eat them. If the litter is very large it is probably wise to try to remove the later afterbirths as eating too many will give her diarrhoea. However it is natural for her to eat them and she should be allowed some.

Apart from puppies become stuck, the other problem

bitches have is called inertia. This means that the uterus becomes tired and stops contracting. It may happen early on, even during the first stage of labour, particularly in older bitches, or those which are overweight or when the litter is very large or very small, i.e. one big puppy. This is called primary inertia. A green vaginal discharge means that an afterbirth has separated from the wall of the uterus and that puppy is deprived of oxygen, therefore it signals the onset of the second stage of labour, even in a bitch which shows no sign of straining. Your vet may give her injections to encourage the contractions to start again, but usually this is not sufficient and a caesarian operation will be required. Secondary inertia occurs when a bitch is exhausted during the birth of a large litter when the first puppies caused problems. This is more likely to respond to injections but if there are several pups yet to be born, your vet may still recommend a caesarian section.

During whelping, you should offer your bitch a drink periodically, although she is unlikely to want to eat. When you think she is finished, it is a good idea to have your vet come to examine her to check that there are no pups left inside and to give her an injection to make the womb shrink down. If she is long-coated she will be very messy, as will the whelping box, and if you can persuade her to leave her puppies to go outside to urinate, you can put fresh bedding in the box and clean her up a little. It is as

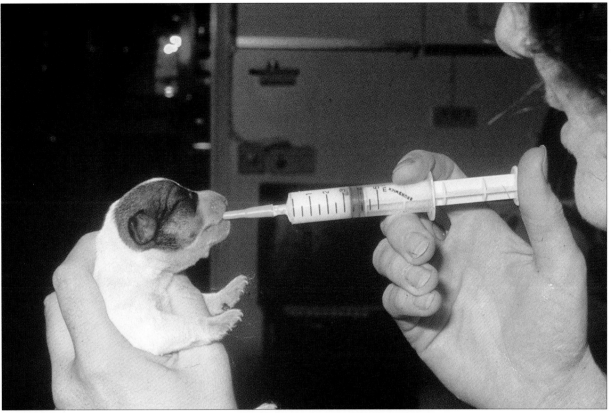

▲ *Hand-rearing: if a newborn puppy cannot suck he can be fed via a stomach tube.*

well to trim off long hair on the bitch's tail and hind-quarters before the whelping to make it easier to clean her up afterwards. She will grow a completely new coat after whelping anyway. She will continue to produce a dark brown discharge for a week or two after the birth – if it is any other colour or smelly, this is abnormal and she should be examined right away by your vet.

When she is settled again in her box with her pups she can be offered something light to eat – milk, scrambled egg, a little chicken or fish is suitable. Over the next few days her diet should be gradually increased and she should be fed at least four times daily. Bitches with large litters may even need feeding during the night. By two weeks after whelping she should be eating at least three or four times her normal amount of food.

Although she will not want to leave her pups, she should be made to go outside several times per day. However, she should not be taken for walks in case she brings back infection to them. Some bitches are better mothers than others – fortunately, most love their pups but a few are not really interested. Even so your bitch should appear reasonably content and she should be eating well by four or five days after whelping. If she seems anxious, restless, wanting to go outside, scrabbling about with a fading appetite – these are danger signals and you should contact your vet without delay.

Your vet should remove the puppies' dew claws by the time they are three days old, and the tails if you wish them to be docked. However some vets are unwilling to do this.

REARING, WEANING AND SELLING PUPPIES

A good brood bitch, well fed, will do all the work for you for the first two or three weeks. The puppies' eyes open at 10 days and they should be gaining weight rapidly. If one appears to be falling behind the others it may have a defect, for example, a cleft palate. In a large litter it may simply be pushed out by the other puppies and it will be the runt. Even if it seems otherwise well, it is a good idea to let your vet examine a small puppy as you do not want to sell it to someone if it has a problem, e.g. a heart defect.

Healthy puppies sleep most of the time except when they are hungry, when they crawl about making lusty cries or humming like bees. A sick puppy feels limp in your hand and crawls slowly about, moaning. Often the bitch pushes it away as though she no longer wants it. Very occasionally whole litters die very young – this is known as 'fading puppy syndrome'. The causes are still unknown and it is very sad for any breeder. Cold contrib-

BREEDING A LITTER

THE FIRST WEEKS OF LIFE

▲ At one week old these Cavalier King Charles puppies are still blind and deaf, but plump and active. Eyes will open at 10 days.

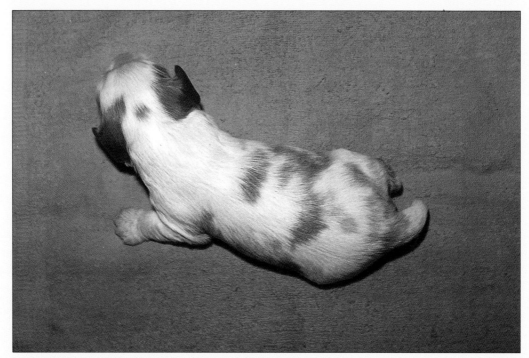

▲ At two weeks, this puppy, eyes now open, begins to explore the whelping box.

▲ At three weeks, although a little unsteady on his legs, he is able to move about and becoming playful. This is a delightful age. Worming and weaning should now begin.

▲ At five weeks, he is eating well, running about and playing, though still sucking from his dam several times daily.

utes to it, so make sure the temperature is high enough if the puppies seem unhappy. With a large litter, it may mean that the bitch does not have enough milk or that she is not letting them feed. Puppies' nails are very sharp and some bitches' teats become very sore. This is easily corrected by nipping off the very ends of the nails with scissors.

If you are unlucky, either because the bitch dies or is too ill, or the litter is too large, you may have to hand-rear some puppies. Nowadays, excellent bitch milk replacer powder is made by several manufacturers and your vet or pet shop should be able to supply it. The milk should be fed at blood heat every two hours day and night, made up with water according to the manufacturer's instructions. Very young puppies cannot suck an artificial teat very well and you may have to drop the milk onto the tongue. A small baby's bottle may be used once the puppies can suck and you will soon learn when a puppy has had enough. It will make treading movements on your lap as it would when feeding from the bitch and you will need to imitate the action of the bitch's tongue by rubbing the abdomen to make it pass urine. Once each pup is clean it can be returned to the box which should have a hot water bottle in it, wrapped in towels. By the third-week, three-hourly feeding is sufficient and the puppies can be taught to lap from a saucer.

All puppies should be ready to start a little solid food at about three weeks. Some breeders use baby food but finely minced beef is the food puppies take most readily. Once daily is adequate to begin with, increasing gradually to four or five small meals daily. As soon as the puppies are lapping milk and eating readily, a prepared balanced puppy food should be introduced to encourage correct bone growth. As stated in the chapter on caring for your puppy, the usual regime is two meat and biscuit meals and two or three milk and cereal meals. If you prefer to use a home-prepared diet this should be as varied as possible with a mineral/vitamin supplement added to it.

Meat is very deficient in calcium, so you will have problems if too much meat is fed with insufficient minerals. Sterilized bone flour is cheap and you are unlikely to do much harm with it, but some puppies do not like it therefore calcium tablets should be given instead. From two to four weeks, the drain on the bitch's calcium reserves is at its greatest therefore she would also benefit from calcium tablets.

At three weeks and again at five weeks, all the puppies and the bitch should be wormed. You vet will supply the medication. You may be surprised how many worms the

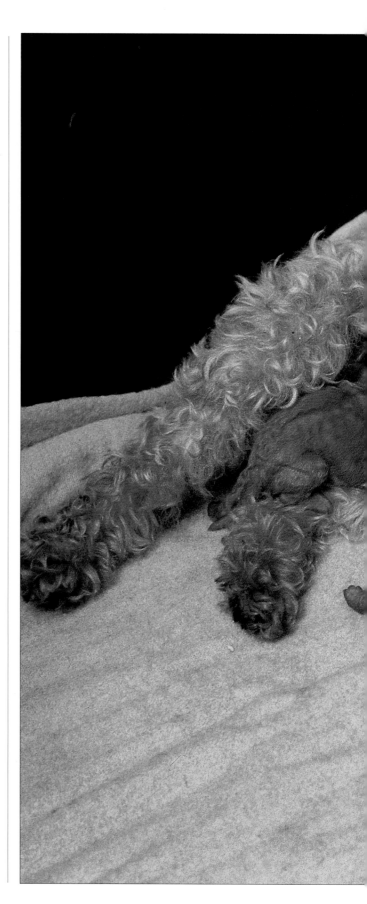

► *A young litter of five Poodle puppies feed hungrily from their dam.*

▲ *The Poodle puppies should now be almost weaned and drinking water, but still need their dam occasionally for comfort, play and discipline.*

▶ *Children love to play with puppies, like these young Rottweilers, but make sure they wash their hands afterwards and understand that puppies can be easily hurt if roughly handled.*

puppies pass – if they are heavily infested they should be wormed again before being sold, especially if they are going to families with children.

By three weeks the puppies will be trying to scramble out of the whelping box, so the front should be removed. By four weeks they will be running about, learning to use their legs, and playing. From this stage until six weeks, they become very hard work as they are extremely mischievous, but they are adorable and great fun. The routine of cleaning up, feeding and rescuing them from potentially dangerous situations is a full-time job, and although you will enjoy it, you will also be thinking hard about finding them new homes, as you collapse into a chair for a well-earned rest. By now, the bitch will be a little tired of them and she will want to stay with them less and less. However a good brood bitch will play with her puppies and discipline them, feeding them periodically when they are most insistent and bringing up her food for them if you do not feed her elsewhere.

The best way to sell puppies is through contacts from other breeders – most are prepared to pass on requests from potential buyers if they do not have puppies themselves. You should certainly inform breed club secretaries

that you have a litter, saying how many dogs and bitches you have. Sadly, there is often a glut of puppies at certain times of the year but if you are lucky and yours are the only pups around, you should have no trouble selling them. You should try to avoid having pups for sale around Christmas but if you cannot help it, it is unwise to allow anyone to collect a puppy just before Christmas Day. Apart from the danger of it being an unwanted present, a busy household on Christmas Day is not the best place for a confused and possibly frightened puppy.

If you have no breed contacts you will have to rely on advertising. To save money, the advertisement should be concise and accurate, therefore you should word it carefully. It is probably wise to put in the price you want, which saves phone calls from people only wanting to ask the price. Unfortunately many people telephone and make appointments to come to see puppies, and then do not arrive, so try not to be upset if it happens. When potential buyers do come, weigh them up carefully – you do not have to sell them a puppy if you think they are unsuitable. Good homes are what you want for your puppies, where they will be loved and well cared for. This should be your prime consideration.

CHAPTER SEVEN

The Sick or Injured Dog

An injured dog needs to be carried with great care, here supported along his whole body.

WHAT IS NORMAL?

The normal healthy dog is mainly interested in food and walks, though the reproductive urges are strong and may take precedence from time to time. This is especially noticeable in the bitch for about eight weeks after oestrus when she may go slightly off her food and become mopey, sometimes producing milk and 'mothering' toys or woolly hats. The male dog may go completely off his food for several days and become restless, with a tendency to whine or even howl, if there is a bitch in oestrus nearby. Behaviour like this may cause the caring owner much anxiety but it is natural and the dog will not have any other signs of illness.

The healthy dog has a glossy or springy coat, not dry but not excessively oily either. His eyes are bright, he has an alert expression, a pink tongue (except for the Chow which normally has a pigmented tongue) and, usually, the traditional sign of good condition – a cold, wet nose. However, there are many healthy dogs with dry noses. In the days prior to vaccination, a nose which was crusty with a discharge was a sign of that most widespread and

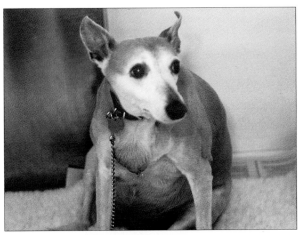

▲ *This dog has several problems, but the main one is obesity.*

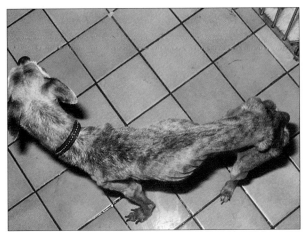

▲ *An extreme case of emaciation.*

▲ *The normal male posture for urination.*

feared disease, distemper, hence the emphasis on the appearance of the nose by dog owners.

Ideal body condition varies depending on the amount of exercise or work the dog performs, and on his conformation, but usually one can feel the ribs but not see them. In the long-coated breeds, assessment of body fat is best done by feel in any case. The dog will put on weight first just behind the shoulder blades and then across the back. Spayed bitches and castrated dogs often have solid pads of fat on either side of the loins. If you can feel the ribs, back and hip bones easily through the skin the dog is probably too thin and the cause should be determined. However if he is young, and otherwise well, he is better on the thin side – dogs are much like humans when it comes to middle-age spread! Some large breeds of the hound and gundog groups may carry very little fat when young, particularly Greyhounds, Salukis and Setters.

Male dogs urinate very frequently when out for walks, usually lifting one hind leg. This is normal and used for territory scent-marking. Male puppies squat like bitches until about nine months to one year, when they are sexually mature. Squatting and straining in a dog which normally lifts his leg is very abnormal and is an indication to seek veterinary advice, but a few dogs never learn to lift their legs at all.

Frequency of passing solid waste (faeces) varies tremendously among normal dogs. The majority pass once or twice daily – more than five times daily is probably abnormal. Consistence of faeces also varies, as does colour, which depends on the type of food eaten. Passing the odd runny motion is perfectly normal, especially as most dogs have a tendency to eat indigestible materials from time to time. Diarrhoea is a body defence mechanism which hastens the passage of noxious material through the gut. It is only serious if severe or persistent, accompanied by dehydration or weight loss. Unfortunately, diarrhoea is inconvenient in a house-trained dog because he may not be able to reach the garden in time, and a nasty mess is the result.

Similarly, vomiting may also be classed as a normal activity for dogs. If material eaten is totally indigestible, the body will reject it very quickly. Dogs are well known for eating grass, supposedly to make themselves sick, although fresh young grass is greatly enjoyed by many dogs as an addition to their diet. Bitches with puppies will regurgitate food. The puppies eat this readily and it is nature's way of weaning them on to solid food. Greedy dogs which gorge themselves will also vomit back food and then eat it again. However, persistent or regular vomiting can be a sign of serious illness.

Sneezing and coughing may also be normal – just think how often you yourself sneeze or cough. These are the body's response to irritation of the respiratory system. Once again 'Is it normal?' becomes 'How often?' In short-faced dogs, noisy breathing may be normal but in most dogs it is not. Occasionally a dog may snort and appear to choke – these attacks may distress the dog when they occur but if they are short and the dog is normal afterwards, this is probably what is known as reverse sneezing. It is associated with irritation in the back of the nose. Any dogs with a long soft palate (the tissue which separates the nose from the mouth) are especially prone to it.

The normal dog has a slight watery discharge from the nose, an occasional brown crust in the corners of the eyes and clean ears. Certain breeds have runny eyes because of faulty conformation (narrow tear ducts, extra eyelashes touching the eyeball and so on). Ear trouble may result from fine hair growing in the ear canal (e.g., in Poodles) or in those breeds with floppy ears, where there is poor ear ventilation (e.g., Spaniels and Labradors). You should watch out for discharge, which may be dark brown or yellow, and for evidence of scratching, head-shaking or holding the head to one side. The old-fashioned term for ear trouble of any kind is canker, but the word is seldom used now.

Scratching of the skin occasionally is normal. However, once again it is a matter of degree. Most skin trouble in dogs is caused by parasites, particularly fleas, so keep a look out for them when grooming. Bald patches and scabs should be investigated.

Discharge from the front passage or vulva is normal when a bitch is in season and after whelping and a few bitches may have a slight discharge at other times which will cause them to lick the area. Treatment is unnecessary unless she is off her food, drinking excessively or vomiting, when veterinary assistance is essential. Male dogs usually have a greenish discharge from the sheath and this may be quite copious. It is normal and does not require treatment unless there is evidence of irritation, or unless blood is present.

Excessive drinking is a sign of great concern to dog owners as it may be associated with several serious conditions. However it may be simply a nervous habit and is normal in hot weather or after strenuous exercise.

SIGNS OF ILL-HEALTH

To summarize, signs which require veterinary attention are as follows:
- Loss of appetite
- Listlessness
- Irritation of the eyes/ears or discharge from them
- Thick discharge from the nose
- Persistent sneezing
- Frequent coughing
- Difficulty in breathing
- Bleeding from any orifice
- Persistent vomiting or diarrhoea
- Difficulty in passing urine or motions
- Fits or collapsing episodes
- Lameness or paralysis of limbs
- Drinking excessively
- Persistent scratching or biting at the skin
- Excessive coat loss producing bare patches
- Abdominal swelling
- Unexplained weight loss
- Whelping difficulty – see chapter on breeding

SIGNS REQUIRING EMERGENCY TREATMENT

One of the most important aspects of good veterinary care is the speed with which you can obtain assistance in a genuine emergency. In countries where veterinary surgeons are required to provide a 24-hour service, this should not be a problem, but you should make sure what the procedure is in case you ever need to use it.

Of course, you should also show consideration for your vet by not abusing this service. It is amazing but true that people will telephone in the middle of the night to enquire about vaccination or boarding kennels! If you are always disturbing your vet with trivialities, you cannot expect him or her to be very receptive when you have a real problem. Vets are human and have their private lives also – when they are on duty during the night, they often have no time off during the day to compensate for lost sleep: most vets do not work 'shifts'. Therefore it is vital that you should know the signs which indicate a true emergency situation.

■ **ROAD TRAFFIC ACCIDENTS** – any dog which has been hit by a car should receive veterinary attention as soon as possible, even if it appears to be all right. The injured dog

LIFTING AN INJURED DOG

Great care must be taken when moving an injured dog because it is likely to be in pain and may well attempt to bite, so avoid lifting or touching the dog more than necessary. If a blanket is available, use it as a temporary stretcher; two people can hold it level by gripping the four corners.

needs very careful handling, not only to reduce pain but also for owner protection, as even the friendliest dog will bite from fear and shock. The best way to lift an injured dog is to make a stretcher from a blanket or other suitable material. Transferring the dog to the stretcher should be done very gently – unfortunately, this method requires two people.

■ **GASTRIC TORSION (BLOAT)** – this is a condition which affects large and giant breeds of dog, particularly those which are deep-chested. The causes are unknown, although it often occurs at night, after a big meal, and may be a consequence of eating a large amount of spoiled food or rubbish. The signs are a sudden onset of restlessness with attempts to vomit which are unsuccessful, crying, turning the head to look at the flanks, stretching and gradual distension of the abdomen, which feels like a drum. This is one of the most serious emergencies and the only chance of saving the dog is immediate action by your vet.

■ **SERIOUS BLEEDING** – a little blood goes a very long way but really profuse bleeding will soon cause collapse and death if not dealt with. If the cause is a severed blood vessel it may be possible to stop it by external pressure – see 'First Aid'. However, if the dog is coughing, vomiting or passing blood, this is not possible. One common cause is the rodent poison warfarin. The dog will need rapid treatment and possibly a blood transfusion, therefore if you have another dog of reasonable size, take it along too – it may need to be a blood donor. Blood from the stomach or high in the intestine will appear black and tarry, whereas blood from lower down, from the large intestine, will be bright red.

■ **CHOKING OR SUDDEN ONSET OF BREATHING DIFFICULTY** – this may be due to a foreign body becoming stuck in the throat. Dogs should not be allowed to play with small objects or sharp sticks. You may have to try to remove it yourself if things are desperate, otherwise you should try to reach the vet as soon as possible. With any breathing problem have a careful look at the colour of the tongue (watch your fingers). If it is mauve or purple, you should obtain help immediately. Puncture wounds in the side of the chest which are accompanied by progressive breathing difficulty are also very serious, although they may not look very bad initially.

■ **PROLONGED FITS** – any fit is frightening enough for most owners to make them ring the vet straight away. However, even if your dog is a known epileptic, prolonged fits, or a series of fits running into one another, need emergency treatment. This condition is known as *status epilepticus* and it may be fatal if not controlled. A bitch rearing puppies may become hyperexcitable and go into convulsions because of low blood calcium level (eclampsia); this is also an emergency but it is easy to treat if caught early.

Fainting may occur for a variety of reasons, one of which may be a heart problem. You should call the vet as soon as possible though the chances are that the dog will have recovered by the time the vet sees him, and in these cases the cause may be very difficult to establish.

Dogs may collapse on a hot day due to heat stroke,

THE SICK OR INJURED DOG

especially if left in cars. This is a dire emergency but if you recognize the cause you can apply first aid (see later).

■ **VERY SEVERE VOMITING AND/OR DIARRHOEA** – Veterinary advice should be sought within 12 hours of the onset. Do not give the dog anything to eat or drink.

FIRST AID

First aid may help to save your dog but it must be applied correctly, otherwise it may do more harm than good.

■ **BLEEDING** – Dogs frequently cut themselves, usually on glass, when out for walks. Most cuts, especially on the feet, are not serious. The bleeding is bright red and profuse initially but soon slows down to a trickle. A bandage will help keep it clean if you have suitable material handy. The technique is not difficult to master and it is useful to learn to apply a bandage before you need to do it. A clean pad, such as a handkerchief, kept on with a sock tied above the foot is also effective. Wounds should be carefully cleaned with warm water and gentle dabbing with clean cotton wool to remove grit and dirt. Hair is also a problem with dog wounds and trimming round the edges is advisable. If a cut is more than ½ in (1.3 cm) long, it may require stitching and this should be done by your vet, within 24 hours if possible.

▲ *Young dogs suffer from incomplete or 'green stick' fractures which may be treated with a heavy bandage or plaster cast.*

If a blood vessel has been severed, bleeding will be persistent, dark red if from a vein and bright red and spurting, in time with the heart beats, if from an artery Arterial bleeding is serious. Tourniquets are now considered to be dangerous, so the best first aid treatment is to put a clean pad onto the wound and apply pressure. If the wound is on a limb, the area should be bandaged tightly, right down to the toes if the wound is not on the foot. When blood seeps through, another pad and another bandage should be applied on top. This should be repeated as often as necessary to slow the bleeding until you reach the vet. A dog which has been hit by a car should be handled as little as possible to minimize the risk of further internal injury and pain from fractures, except for lifting him into a car as previously described. However, if handling is essential, a badly broken leg should be supported, if possible by wrapping round it layers of thick soft material, ideally cotton wool, well above and below the site of the break. A piece of rigid material such as wood may be included in the wrapping to form a splint, but preferably not next to the skin.

If the dog is unconscious, his tongue should be pulled forward, and he should be positioned with the nose in line with the neck and the head lower than the body, so that any vomit will tend to run out of the mouth.

Artificial respiration is not very successful in dogs except in newborn puppies, and chest compression should not be attempted in road accident cases, where there may be broken ribs. In smaller dogs or those with narrow chests, external heart massage can be applied by squeezing both sides of the chest wall behind the elbows, and you might be able to apply mouth-to-mouth artificial respiration if you cup your fingers around the sides of the mouth. Naturally you would only try this in desperate circumstances.

Dogs which appear to have collapsed with heat stroke ideally should be immersed in cold water as soon as possible. If a clinical thermometer is available, the temperature is recorded by inserting it into the rectum (back passage), preferably after lubricating it with vaseline or liquid paraffin. In the normal dog the rectal temperature is around 101.5°F (38.6°C). In heat stroke the temperature may be as high as 110°F (43.3°C). If it is not possible to immerse the dog in water, ice may be applied to the skin, especially to the head, or the dog may be covered with wet towels. Care should be taken not to let the temperature go too low.

■ **POISONING** – Signs of poisoning in dogs are usually those of effects on the gut or the brain. If the dog is already showing signs there is little you can do except call the vet. If he is having fits, you should keep him from injuring himself by confining him in a darkened room until help arrives.

SIMPLE MEDICAL PRECAUTIONS FOR THE DOG OWNER

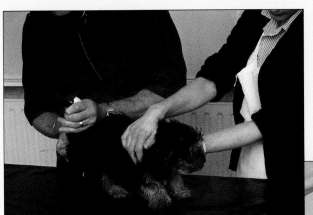

TAKING THE TEMPERATURE First shake down the thermometer and lubricate the bulb with liquid paraffin or vaseline. Enlist the help of an assistant to hold the dog, and carefully insert the thermometer into the rectum while holding the tail with the other hand. Leave for one minute and do not let go of the thermometer.

TABLET ADMINISTRATION Dogs are expert at spitting out tablets. Hold the head up and push the tablet as far down the throat as possible.

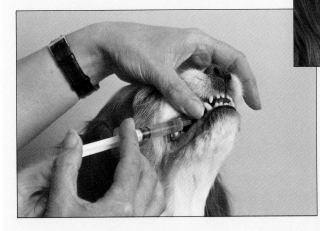

ADMINISTRATION OF LIQUID MEDICINE Using a syringe, obtained from your vet, hold the head up and squirt the liquid slowly into the side of the mouth or into a pouch of lip at the corner of the mouth.

However, if a dog is seen to eat something which you suspect will harm him, you can make him vomit. The best method is to give a crystal of washing soda which usually induces vomiting very quickly. If washing soda is not available, mustard or a strong salt solution may be effective. Poisoning with caustic (burning) materials such as strong acid or alkali is very unlikely to occur in dogs, but under these circumstances it is best *not* to induce vomiting. In all cases of suspected poisoning you should seek veterinary advice without delay.

Burns to the outside of the body are usually caused by scalding with hot liquid due to a pan falling on the dog from the stove. These burns are always more serious in heavy-coated breeds because the coat holds the heat. Cold running water should be poured onto the area as quickly as possible, for at least ten minutes.

NURSING

Many cases which were thought by vets to be hopeless have been saved by devoted owners who were prepared to nurse their dogs back to health

The principles of good nursing are just the same in dogs as in humans – keeping the patient warm and clean, and ensuring that sufficient fluids and tempting foods are offered at suitable intervals. Wounds usually need daily dressing and drugs should be administered correctly. Your vet will advise you, and will show you how to administer tablets and liquid medicine. These techniques are not always as easy as they look and are better practised before you need to use them in earnest.

Soft bedding material is available which is relatively non-absorbent, allowing urine to pass through to news-

111

THE SICK OR INJURED DOG

▲ *Ear trouble is extremely common in dogs. Here a veterinary surgeon examines a dog's ear using an auroscope.*

paper beneath. This is ideal for canine patients. If unable to rise, dogs should be turned frequently to avoid bed-sores. Paralyzed dogs, or those with injuries which would benefit from mild exercise, require gentle physiotherapy and massage, using a towel round the abdomen to lift them. They need plenty of encouragement, too, and no veterinary treatment can replace tender loving care.

PREVENTING COMMON PROBLEMS

If you are fortunate, one visit per year to the vet for examination, re-vaccination and worming is all that your dog will need. However if your dog is prone to particular problems, more frequent visits may be recommended. Three common reasons are as follows:

■ **NAIL CLIPPING** – large dogs which take plenty of exercise very rarely need any attention to their nails, unless one is split or torn. Most pedigree dogs now have their 'dew claws' (the small fifth claws on the inside of the legs) removed soon after birth, but if these are present, they should be kept short to prevent them from curling round and growing into the skin. Small dogs may need nail clipping periodically – you can learn to do it yourself but it is very easy to clip too far back, especially when the nails are black, so many owners prefer their vet to do it.

THE PARALYZED DOG

Dogs often suffer from spinal injuries or disc disease. If the damage to the spinal cord is not too severe the dog may recover, but it will take at least six weeks during which time he will need intensive nursing. Bladder function and the prevention of bed sores are the main concerns.

▓ **ANAL GLAND PROBLEMS** – it is commonly believed that if a dog rubs its rear end along the ground it has worms. This old wives' tale originated because one type of human parasite causes intense anal itching, but this worm does not affect dogs. The usual reason is that the anal sacs have failed to empty. The dog has two of these small glands beside the anus at 4 and 8 o'clock positions. Each gland only has one small hole through which it empties and should this become blocked the dog will suffer discomfort. If the situation continues, an abscess may form and this is acutely painful. It is a simple job to empty the glands and if the condition recurs, you may learn to do it yourself. Most grooming parlours offer anal gland emptying and nail-clipping as part of their service.

▓ **TEETH CLEANING** – as a dog ages, his teeth, particularly the outer surfaces, become coated with a hard deposit. This material traps bacteria and causes gum disease. In severe cases, the teeth loosen and fall out and many small dogs lose teeth at quite an early age. Dogs hardly, if ever, suffer from tooth decay, unlike humans. It makes sense, therefore, to have the teeth cleaned at regular intervals. It is generally believed that chewing bones helps to keep teeth clean, but their effect is marginal, and as feeding bones may lead to serious problems, most vets suggest that they should not be given. Chop bones and cooked bones, particularly poultry or rabbit bones, are extremely dangerous. Teeth cleaning normally requires an anesthetic but some owners learn to do it themselves and dogs can be quite amenable if accustomed to the procedure from an early age.

▲ *Several types of nail clippers are available including the 'guillotine' variety shown here.*

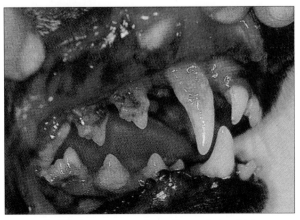

▲ *This is severe case of gum disease in an old dog caused by the build up of tartar on the teeth. The gums have receded exposing the roots, and the teeth are loose.*

SHOWING

CHAPTER EIGHT

Showing

The rewards of months of training and hard work.

GROOMING EQUIPMENT

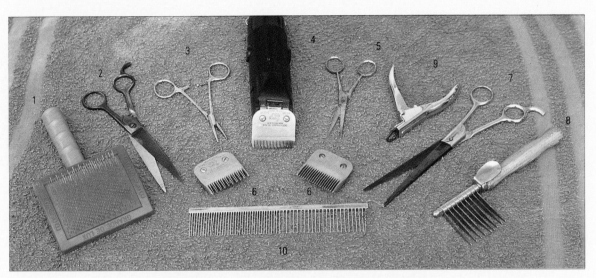

The equipment required for grooming your dog depends on the breed and type of coat, but the following selection should cover most needs: Brush (1) used for smoothing the coat prior to exhibition; trimming scissors can be purchased in various sizes (2, 3, 5, 7); electric clippers (4) are needed for certain breeds which do not shed their coats and various clipper attachments can be purchased (6); nail clippers (9); a very wide-toothed comb (8) should be used for removing tangles, and an all-purpose comb (10) with both wide and narrow gaps between the teeth for general grooming.

THE WORLD OF DOG SHOWING IS controlled in all countries by the Kennel Club of that country which lays down regulations for the running of shows and the registration of pedigree dogs. The aim of showing is to gain for your dog the title of champion, and if you achieve this, you will have the pleasure of knowing that your dog is one of the best specimens of the breed. You will be able to command higher prices for a dog's services at stud or for a bitch's puppies, and the experience you gain will stand you in good stead should you be invited to judge. You will then be able to influence which new dogs become champions and the process comes full circle.

Showing is undoubtedly a competitive activity, but unlike a ball game or a race, the winner is not chosen by any objective criteria. When you show your dog you are asking for a judge's opinion, and his opinion may be very different from someone else's. Therefore, even if the same dogs are shown repeatedly, the results are bound to vary from day to day. However it is not such a lottery as it sounds. Any judge who knows the breed will be familiar with the standard – a description written down by the Kennel Club of that breed, listing the qualities and faults which judges should look for. One person's interpretation of that standard may be slightly different from another's, but if the standard says, for example, that a dog should be 22 inches at the shoulder with almond-shaped dark eyes

and prick ears, you are unlikely to win with a specimen which is 26 inches at the shoulder and has round yellow eyes and drop ears.

It is a good idea to obtain an unbiased opinion of your dog from a well-known breeder or judge. However, you should not necessarily be discouraged if you are told that your dog has faults – the perfect dog has never been bred, and you may find that the other dogs entered on the day have worse faults than yours so that you will end up with a prize after all. The best attitude to take is that a visit to a show is a pleasant day out where you can meet and talk to other people interested in your breed. Then if you win a prize it is a bonus. Show people do not like poor losers.

PREPARATION

Once you have decided to go to a show, the most important thing you have to do is to find out the name and address of the secretary, send for an entry form and fill it in. Entries close well in advance of the show date, often by several weeks, to allow time for catalogue printing, so you should send off your entry and pay the fee in good time.

There are various sizes of shows, from very small to very large. You may feel that you would rather not tackle a

SHOWING

PREPARING FOR THE SHOW

BATHING Wet the coat thoroughly with warm (not hot) water, apply shampoo or mild detergent, lather and then rinse thoroughly. Watch the eyes and ears. For breeds where a harsh coat texture is required, bathe several days prior to the show so that the coat is not too soft on the day.

GROOMING This should be thorough using combs of different types depending on the length of the coat. Finish with a good brushing.

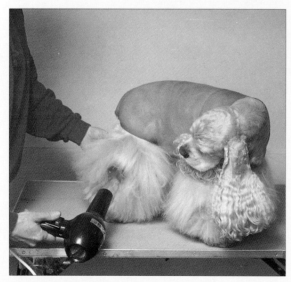

DRYING Thorough drying is essential. Start with warm towels and finish with a hair dryer, brushing at the same time.

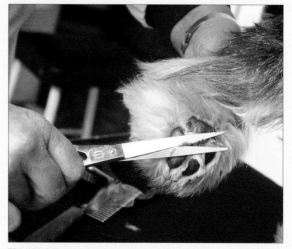

TRIMMING The amount of trimming required depends on the breed. Here the hair between the pads is being removed.

▲ 'Bending' poles and jumps are common obstacles in agility competitions.

big show on a first outing, but the championship shows have several advantages for novice dogs and owners. Firstly, there are more classes, hence your dog is more likely to be judged along with others of his own age and sex – at small shows, classes are often mixed. Secondly, there is usually more space – at the smaller show your puppy may be more likely to be trodden on, or attacked by another dog because they are forced to stand close together. The larger shows usually have 'benching' – wooden benches divided up with metal partitions so that your dog has his own allotted space where he can sit undisturbed, and under cover. Thirdly, big shows attract owners and breeders from all over the country. You will have a chance to see the best dogs and learn from their owners the tricks of the trade. Even if you do not take the dog, it is a good idea to visit any championship show in your area just to watch the judging.

When you fill in your entry form, you will be asked for details about your dog and it is important not to make mistakes. You can be disqualified from winning if someone complains, for instance, the birth date or name of the sire or dam appeared wrongly in the catalogue, and this was due to your error. You will be required to put down the numbers of the classes which you wish to enter, but do not enter too many. Three are probably enough, as your dog may be rather tired or bored after these. There are usually special classes for young and old dogs defined by age. Apart from these, entries are decided by the number of classes which a dog has won previously – a sort of handicap system. You can also enter variety classes, where you compete with dogs of other breeds. These are great fun, although wins do not count towards a championship or any other title.

Once you have entered the show, you should work

SHOWING

SHOWING

hard to polish the early training which you should have carried out – walking well on the leash, standing still (on a table if a small dog), being handled by strangers and learning not to be distracted by other dogs.

As the show date approaches, you will need to think about how you can improve the dog's appearance. You are not permitted to use chalk or any other material on the coat which could be construed as altering its colour, so most people give their dogs a thorough bath several days before, especially if light-coloured. It is best not to do it too close to the day of the show if your dog is required to have a harsh stand-off coat. Too recent shampooing will make the coat soft and therefore three or four days before is ideal.

Before the bath, the dog should be groomed to remove any dead hair. You should make sure that you have sufficient old towels to dry him with afterwards. The water should be warm but not hot and a spray attachment for the tap is helpful – failing that you will need a jug or small bucket from which to pour water over him. First, wet the coat thoroughly and then add the shampoo, working it well in to the coat, being careful to avoid the ears and eyes. You can use special dog shampoo which your vet or pet shop will supply, or you can use very diluted mild dishwashing detergent. The main problem with the latter is rinsing the suds out of the coat. Once the dog is well rinsed, you then start to dry him with towels. If he will tolerate it, a long-coated dog should be dried with a hairdryer, brushing the coat with the other hand. Talcum powder can be applied to wavy hair behind the ears to help dry it, provided you brush it all out afterwards. This gives the ears a delightful fluffy appearance. Most dogs enjoy being bathed once they are used to it but if yours decides to be difficult, you will have to enlist help to hold it. To protect the dog's ears you could use cotton-wool earplugs but remember to remove them afterwards.

Breeds which require trimming or stripping usually have this done at the same time. Skilful attention to the coat can enhance a dog's chances of winning considerably, whereas a poor job can ruin a good dog's appearance. Therefore until you are experienced, it is wise to leave this to a professional. Terriers usually have their coats plucked with the fingers, rather than clipped.

Naturally, your dog should be healthy when you take him to a show. No veterinary inspection is carried out at dog shows nowadays, but the judges will not be impressed by fleas, dirty teeth, long nails or runny eyes. If the dog develops any symptoms shortly before the show, such as coughing or diarrhoea, you should leave him at home – it is not fair on the dog or the other exhibitors to risk spreading infection.

◀ *Judging of the Toy group at Crufts Dog Show: a Yorkshire Terrier is being examined.*

SHOWING

THE DAY OF THE SHOW

When the big day arrives, you will be up early, hopefully with everything having been prepared the night before. Your dog should have a nice collar and leash, and you should bring grooming tools, a clean blanket, a towel, water and a bowl, and probably food for coming home late. You will also need titbits to attract your dog's attention at crucial moments in the ring, for big shows a benching chain, and if you have been sent an entry pass, do not forget to take it with you. For yourself, you will need reasonably smart though practical and comfortable clothes. Dog show food is not usually very good, so most exhibitors take a packed lunch. You will also need a clip or pin with which to attach your ring number to your jacket, so that the ring steward can identify you.

Once you arrive at the show, make sure you can find your car again in the parking lot and then follow the

other exhibitors into the showground, showing your pass at the gate if required. Ask a show official where the ring (and benching if supplied) is situated for your breed. Once you and your dog are settled, you can put the final touches to his grooming but be alert for the steward calling your class into the ring. Dogs are always judged before bitches and young dogs before older ones; therefore, if you have a puppy you may be judged at 10 o'clock in the morning, but if you have an older bitch you may not be in the ring until four o'clock in the afternoon.

Once your class has been called, go into the ring and collect your number from the steward. Try not to be nervous as you will communicate this to the dog, and remember, you are there to enjoy yourself!

▲ *Every dog exhibitor's ambition is to reach the final judging in a major dog show. The winner of this Utility group will go forward to compete for 'Best in Show'.*

THE OLD DOG

CHAPTER NINE

The Old Dog

*The fading colour on the head of this Golden
Retriever is a typical sign of ageing in a dog.*

PROBLEMS OF OLD AGE AND SPECIAL CARE

Old age varies greatly with breed – a Great Dane is old at eight years whereas a Border Collie may still be running around a farmyard at 16. As a general rule, small dogs are longer lived than large dogs.

It is said that old age does not come alone. The joints become stiff and the muscles weak – the old dog does not want to run about, climb stairs or jump the way he used to. He may have heart trouble, kidney failure or cancer, and because he does not exercise so much, he may be over-weight, which makes other problems worse. He probably needs a special diet and supplies of tablets, he may be incontinent and he spends longer sleeping.

However there is a special joy in caring for an old dog. He is a great friend; you know each other very well indeed. Any extra work involved is balanced by the fact that he is more sensible and reliable. Many old dogs become very imperious, just like old people, demanding attention and refusing to be ignored, but no one minds – you make allowances because he is old. If the dog is losing his hearing you both adapt to hand signals, and if he is going blind you talk to him more and keep him in surroundings he knows as much as possible. Walks become more leisurely – no more frantic dashing about, but a gentle stroll from one interesting smell to the next. Old dogs like routine. Even so, it is a mistake to think that he does not need mental stimulation. Like all dogs, he will love going somewhere different from time to time and it may surprise you how much he will run about. Even if a dog is unable to exercise he will enjoy going with you in the car, rather than being left alone at home. Old dogs become very dependent and this is perhaps what makes them so endearing.

Frequent veterinary check-ups are necessary and your vet will advise you about diet. The older dog generally does better with two meals per day instead of one, as his intestines do not work so efficiently, and he may benefit from a vitamin/mineral supplement. If there is any hint of kidney trouble, you will be advised to cut down on meat and other protein food and increase the amount of starchy foods and fats. Dogs with heart trouble should be fed on muscle meat rather than offal, and should not be given salty foods. The overweight dog may have to be dieted quite strictly – there are several proprietary weight-reducing diets available for dogs, but it is important to remember that even these, given in excess, will cause the dog to put on weight, and you should not use any other food in addition. Most dogs put on weight through being given scraps or titbits, therefore you should keep the dog out of the kitchen when food is being prepared, and out of the dining room at mealtimes.

It is important to keep the dog comfortable by regular attention to teeth, nails and anal glands, and to keep him well-groomed. Take pride in your dog's appearance, even though he no longer looks as beautiful as he once did, and you will enjoy it when someone says to you, 'Goodness, is he really that old? I thought he was much younger!'

LOSING A FRIEND – THE END OF THE ROAD

The major difference between human and veterinary medicine is the question of euthanasia. This book is not the place for a moral discussion on the rights and wrongs of it. Many people do not believe in it under any circumstances. However, there is no doubt that when an animal is suffering from incurable disease, most owners and vets feel a profound sense of relief that euthanasia is an option open to them.

Even so, if a decision has to be made, it is never easy. It must be the owner's decision and all the vet can do is to offer advice. No one should feel embarrassed about being upset when an animal is dying – research has shown that people react in the same way with an animal as they would if told that a member of their family was incurably ill. Disbelief, anger, fear and, finally, acceptance are the stages, and if a person is pushed into making a decision too quickly, he or she may feel guilty for months afterwards, wondering if it was the right thing to do. 'How will I know when it is the right time?' is the question most people ask. The answer lies in the animal's behaviour – if you know your dog, there will be no problem. You will know when he is no longer enjoying life, when he no longer wants to live. They live only for the moment, therefore you should not worry about staying with them when the deed is done. It is carried out very quickly, an intrave-

▲ *Having a puppy may help you to get over the loss of the older dog.*

THE OLD DOG

nous injection of an overdose of anaesthetic. Most vets will let you stay if you wish but if you become upset, you will upset the dog and this may be worse than leaving him with kind strangers. It is probably ideal for the dog if the vet comes to your house, but it is often not practical and the vet may make a better job of it in the office or surgery, where there is plenty of assistance.

Disposal of the body afterwards is a problem which causes owners anxiety. Vets are happy to take care of this for you and the bodies are usually cremated, although not individually. If you wish the ashes to be returned to you, special arrangements have to be made and it will depend what services are available in your area. If you are able to bury the dog in your garden, it often helps children to come to terms with their loss if you have a little funeral service. In certain areas, there are pet cemeteries where your dog will have a permanent memorial in the form of a little stone or a rose bush. No one should feel ashamed to grieve for a dead animal and it may take some time before you are ready to look for another dog.

The loss is easier to bear if you have another dog and some people buy a puppy when they know that their older dog does not have long to live. This action may have several drawbacks, however. It means extra work with a puppy at a time when the other dog needs attention, and the older one may be jealous of a bouncy pup – indeed it may be very unfair to subject him to this situation, especially if he is ill. On the other hand, your dog may enjoy the company – there is no way of knowing without trying it, but the puppy should be returned if things do not work out. Often the younger dog will pine for a while when the older dog dies, therefore you may find yourself buying him a companion!

Losing a canine friend is a heart-breaking experience for most of us. It is so upsetting that some people say that they will never have another dog. They should remember the pleasures that the dog gave them, however – they far outweigh the sadness.

Rudyard Kipling expressed his feelings in the following touching poem:

"When the body that lived at your single will,
When the whimper of welcome is stilled (how
  still),
When the spirit that answered your every mood
Is gone – wherever it goes – for good,
You will discover how much you care,
And will give your heart to a dog to tear!"

◀ *The years go by but the appetite doesn't diminish!*
The author's bitch on her 13th birthday.

Index

Figures in italics refer to picture captions.

A

adult dogs, 45, 73–4, 76, 79–80, 83–4, 86–7
    see also elderly dogs
            puppies
Afghan Hounds, 32, 34
agility trials, 83, 83, 84, 117
    see also trials
Airedales, 17
Alaskan Malamutes, 23, 25
Alsatians see German Shepherd Dogs
American Cocker Spaniels, 31, 58
anal glands, 113
Australian Terriers, 20

B

Basset Hounds, 32, 34
bathing, 52, 78, 79, 116
Beagles, 32, 35
Bedlington Terriers, 17, 18
behavioural problems, 11, 70–1
    see also social behaviour
            training
birth see whelping
bitches, 14, 45, 59, 89, 108
    breeding, 43, 44, 45, 88, 89–91,
        91–5, 93, 95, 97–9, 97–102, 102,
        104, 104
    gestation periods, 91
    mating, 90, 91, 91, 93
    neutering, 14, 70
    oestrus, 14, 69–70, 76, 79, 91, 107
    pregnancies, 70, 91, 92, 93
    whelping, 79, 94, 97–9
    see also dogs (males)
bleeding, 109, 110
bloat see gastric torsion
Bloodhounds, 32
boarding kennels, 11, 86, 87
body condition see health
body language, 73
body temperature, 87, 97
body weight, 59, 70, 74, 107, 107
bone diseases, 59
    see also diseases
bones, 74, 74
Border Collies, 8, 26, 27, 123
Border Terriers, 17, 17
Borzois, 32, 34
Boston Terriers, 19, 35
bowel actions, 11, 47, 49, 52, 102,

107–8, 107
    see also house training
            hygiene
Boxers, 28, 28
Brachycephalic breeds see short-
    nosed breeds
breeding, 43, 44, 45, 88, 89–91, 91–5,
    93, 95, 97–9, 97–102, 102, 104, 104
    see also pedigrees
breeds, 14, 115
    crosses, 38, 40, 44
    giant, 38, 38–9, 59
    gundogs, 28–32, 29–32, 83
    hunting, 17, 32, 33–4, 35, 38, 38
    long-coated, 14, 16, 52, 61, 76, 79,
        98–9
    setters, 31, 32
    sheepdogs, 8, 10, 25, 25–7, 27, 58,
        123
    short-coated, 52
    short-nosed, 35, 37–8, 78
    Spitz, 16, 16, 21, 22–4, 25
    terriers, 15, 16, 17, 17–20, 21, 35,
        119
    toys, 13, 14–16, 15, 58
Buhunds see Norwegian Buhunds
Bull Terriers, 19
Bulldogs, 35, 36
burial, 125

C

calcium, 102
canine distemper, 55
    see also diseases
car journeys, 45, 65, 65, 68–9, 86, 87,
    87
    see also transportation
carrying cages, 61, 68
    see also transportation
castration, 58, 70
    see also neutering
cats:
    and dogs, 11
Cavalier King Charles Spaniels, 16, 29,
    31, 59, 98, 100
chewing, 46, 74, 74
Chihuahuas, 16
    long-coated, 14
children:
    and dogs, 7, 10, 25, 44, 44, 74, 104
choice:
    of dog, 11, 43–5
choke chains, 80, 81
    see also collars and leashes
choking, 109
claws, 99, 112, 113
coats, 107
    see also grooming

Cocker Spaniels, 31, 49, 50, 58
collars and leashes, 10–11, 61–2, 63,
    66, 80
    choke chains, 80, 81
collies see sheepdogs
colostrum, 94
    see also whelping
commands, 62–3, 66, 69
    see also obedience
commercial dog food, 49–50, 73–4
    see also feeding
companionship, 6, 7, 11, 14, 16, 123,
    125
competitions see trials
Corgis, 27, 27
costs, 10, 11, 38
coughing, 108
cremation, 125
crossbreeds, 38, 40, 44
    see also breeds
Crufts Dog Show, 72, 119

D

dealers, 43–4
death, 99, 102, 125
defects:
    in-bred, 89, 90, 90
    see also diseases
diet see feeding
diseases, 25, 27, 44, 54, 55–6, 89
    bone diseases, 59
    inbred, 27, 28, 31–2, 35, 89
    kennel cough, 87
    parasite control, 55–6
    rabies, 84
    vaccinations, 44, 54, 55, 87
    see also health
            injuries
distemper see canine distemper
docking, 99
dog kennels, 52
dog-guards, 65, 65, 68
    see also transportation
dogs (males), 14, 45, 59, 76
    castration, 58, 70
    mating, 90, 91, 91, 93
    studs, 90–1
    see also bitches
dogs' homes, 44, 45
drink, 45, 74, 98, 102, 108
    see also feeding

E

ear mites, 56
ears, 58, 78, 112, 119
elderly dogs, 122–3, 123, 125, 125
    see also adult dogs
elderly people:

and dogs, 6, 10, 14
Elkhounds see Norwegian Elkhounds
English Cocker Spaniels, 49
English Setters, 31, 72
English Springer Spaniels, 29
equipment, 10–11, 45, 45, 61, 115, 120
euthanasia, 123, 125
exercise, 11, 12, 65, 80, 83, 95
    see also walking
external parasites, 56
eyes, 89, 89

F

fading puppy syndrome, 99, 102
false pregnancies, 70, 93
    see also pregnancies
feeding, 14, 16, 31, 38, 43, 45, 47,
    49–50, 50, 58–9, 73–4, 76, 95, 99,
    102, 123
    see also drink
field trials, 83
    see also gun dogs
              trials
fighting, 73
Finnish Spitzs, 23
first aid, 110–11, 111
    see also nursing
fits, 109
fleas, 56
flexi-leads, 62, 66, 80
    see also collars and leashes
flying, 45
    see also transportation
Fox Terriers, 18
Foxhounds, 34, 35
fresh food, 74
    see also feeding

G

gastric torsion, 109
German Shepherd Dogs, 26, 27, 90
gestation periods, 91
    see also pregnancies
giant breeds, 38, 38–9, 59
    see also breeds
Golden Retrievers, 29, 122
Gordon Setters, 31, 32
Great Danes, 11, 38, 39, 123
Greyhounds, 32, 35, 40
grooming, 11, 13, 21, 28, 31, 52, 53, 61,
    61, 76, 76, 78, 79–80, 115–16, 119,
    120–1, 123
    see also bathing
guard dogs, 28, 28
    see also working dogs
guide dogs, 10, 10
    see also working dogs
gundogs, 28–32, 29–32, 83

see also hunting dogs
          working dogs

H

handling see socializing
hand-rearing, 102
    see also weaning
hard pad see canine distemper
health, 107–13, 119, 123
    check-ups, 52–3, 55
    see also diseases
              injuries
heat see oestrus
heat stroke, 109–10
heel-walking, 62–3, 66
    see also walking
hepatitis see infectious canine
          hepatitis
hereditary defects see in-bred defects
hereditary diseases see in-bred
          diseases
hip dysplasia, 89, 90
    see also defects
holidays, 11–12, 84, 86–7, 86
hormone treatments, 70
hotels see holidays
hounds see hunting dogs
house training, 50, 52, 61
    see also bowel actions
              hygiene
human diseases, 10
Hungarian Pulis, 26
Hungarian Vizlas, 31, 32
hunting dogs, 17, 32, 33–4, 35, 38, 38
    see also gundogs
              working dogs
Huskies see Siberian Huskies
hygiene, 11, 16, 47, 83, 87, 104
    see also bowel actions
              house training

I

identity discs, 11
in-bred defects, 89
in-bred diseases, 27, 28, 31–2, 35, 89
    see also diseases
indoor kennels, 52
inertia, 98
infectious canine hepatitis, 55
    see also diseases
injuries, 106, 107–13, 109–10
    see also diseases
              health
insurance, 11
internal parasites, 55–6
intestinal diseases, 54
Irish Setters, 31, 76
Irish Wolfhounds, 38, 38, 40

J

Jack Russell Terriers, 20, 21
Japanese Spitzs, 24

K

Keeshunds, 25, 50
Kennel Clubs, 43, 115
Kennel cough, 87
    see also diseases
kennels see boarding kennels
              dog kennels
              indoor kennels
King Charles Spaniels, 29, 31

L

labour see whelping
Labrador Retrievers, 31, 84, 92, 108
Lakeland Terriers, 19
leashes see collars and leashes
leptospirosis, 55
    see also diseases
lice, 56
line-breeding, 90
    see also breeding
long-coated breeds, 14, 16, 52, 61, 76,
    79, 98–9
    see also breeds
Long-coated Chihuahuas, 14
Lurchers, 40

M

Malamutes see Alaskan Malamutes
Maltese Terriers, 15, 16, 17
mating, 90, 91, 91, 93
    see also breeding
medication, 56, 111, 111
mesh runs, 52
milk, 74, 94, 102
    see also drink
Miniature Poodles, 16
moulting, 76, 79–80
    see also grooming

N

nails see claws
neutering, 14, 70
    see also castration
new homes, 47, 49, 104
Norfolk Terriers, 17, 18
Norwegian Buhunds, 24, 25
Norwegian Elkhounds, 22, 25
Norwich Terriers, 17
noses, 107, 108
nursing, 111–12, 111
    see also first aid

O

obedience, 25, 27, 61–3, 62, 80

INDEX

see also training
obedience trials, 83
  see also trials
obesity *see* body weight
oestrus, 14, 69–70, 76, 79, 91, 107
  see also bitches
old age *see* elderly dogs
Old English Sheepdogs, 27, *27*
older dogs *see* adult dogs
owners, 7

P

paper-training, 50, 52
Papillons, 16, *16*
paralysis, 112, *113*
parsite control, 55–6, 101, 102, 104
  see also diseases
parvovirus, *54*, 55
  see also diseases
pedigrees, 43, 90
  see also breeding
       showing
Pekineses, 16, 36, *37*
pet shops, 43–4
play, 47, *69, 71, 73, 101*
  see also toys
pointers, 31
  see also gun dogs
poisoning, 110–11
police dogs, 8, 10, 27
  see also working dogs
Pomeranians, 16, *16*, 25
Poodles, *53, 61, 76, 95, 102, 104*, 108
  miniatures, 16
  standards, 16
  toys, *13*, 16
pregnancies, 91, *92*, 93
  false, 70, 93
  whelping, *79, 94*, 97–9
protection, 10
Pugs, 36, *36*
punishment, 71
puppies, 11, *41*, 43–5, *43–50*, 47, 49,
  52–3, *53–4*, 55–6, *57–9*, 58–9, 61–3,
  61–3, 65, *65–6*, 68–71, *68–9, 71, 95,
  97, 100–1*
  see also adult dogs
       whelping
Pyrenean Mountain Dogs, 38, *39*

Q

quarantine, 84

R

rabies, 84
  see also diseases

retrievers, *29, 31, 84, 92*, 108, *122*
road accidents *see* traffic conditions
Rottweilers, 28, *28, 43*, 70, *104*
Rough Collies, *25*, 58
roundworms, 55–6, *56*
runs *see* mesh runs

S

St Bernards, 38, *38*
Salukis, 32
Samoyeds, *22*, 25, *57, 79*
scent hounds, 32, *34*, 35
  see also hunting dogs
Scottish Terriers, *15*, 17
scratching, 108
season *see* oestrus
selling puppies, 104
setters, 31, *32*
  see also gundogs
sheepdogs, 8, 10, 25, *25–7, 27*, 58, 123
  see also working dogs
Shih-Tzus, 35, *36*
short-coated breeds, 52, *78*
  see also breeds
short-nosed breeds, 35, *35–7*
showing, 7, 10, 43, 44–5, 61, *68*, 84,
  114, 115, *116–17*, 117, 119–21, *119*,
  121
  see also pedigrees
       trials
Siberian Huskies, *22*
sight hounds, 32, *34*
  see also hunting dogs
skin trouble, 108
  see also health
sleep, 11, 47, *47*, 49, *49*
social behaviour, 25, 28, 38
  see also behavioural problems
socializing, 44, *50*, 52
spaniels, 16, 29, *29*, 31, *37, 59, 98*, 100
spaying *see* neutering
Spitz breeds, 16, *16*, 21, *22–4*, 25
Springer Spaniels, *29, 31*
Standard Poodles, 16
stud dogs, 90–1
teeth, 58, *59*, 113, *113*
temperament, 16, 17, 25, 27, 28, 29, 38,
  44–5
  see also behavioural problems
       social behaviour
terriers, *15*, 16, 17, *17–20*, 21, 35, *119*
Tibetan Spaniels, *37*
the tie, 93
toy breeds, *13*, 14–16, *15*, 58
  see also breeds
Toy Poodles, *13*, 16
toys, 47
  see also play

tracker dogs, 8, 10
  see also working dogs

T

traffic accidents, 108–9
training, 11, 29, 65, *66, 69*, 71, *80–4*,
  83–4, 119
  classes, *84*
  commands, 62–3, 66, 69
  house, 50, 52, 61
  obedience, 25, 27, 61–3, *62*, 80
  show, *68*
trains, 86
  see also transportation
transportation, 45, *61*, 65, *65*, 68–9, 86,
  87, *87*
travel sickness, 45, 68–9
trials
  agility, 83, *83*, 84, *117*
  field, 83
  obedience, 83
  see also showing

U

urination *see* bowel actions

V

vaccinations, 44, *54*, 55, 87
  see also diseases
veterinary care, 11, 44, 45, 52–3, 55,
  108, 123, 125
vitamins, 50, 74, 102
  see also feeding
Vizlas *see* Hungarian Vizlas
vomiting, 108, 110

W

walking, *63*, 65, 80, 123
  to heel, 62–3, *66*
weaning, *101*, 102
weight *see* body weight
Weimaraners, *32*
Welsh Springer Spaniels, *31*
whelping, *79, 94*, 97–9
  see also pregnancies
whelping boxes, *93, 95, 97*, 104
Wire-haired Terriers *see* Fox Terriers
working dogs, 8, 10, *10*, 25, *25–34*,
  27–32, 35, 58, 123
worming, 56, 101, 102, 104
  see also parasite control
       roundworms

Y

Yorkshire Terriers, *15*, 16, 17, *119*